W9-AAV-042

hum♥R for a
teacher's heart

Stories, Quips, and Quotes to Lift the Heart

hum♥R

for a

teacher's heart

Compiled by The Livingstone Corporation

Illustrated by Kristen Myers

HOWARD
PUBLISHING CO.

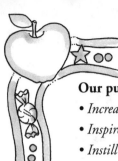

Our purpose at Howard Publishing is to:
- *Increase faith* in the hearts of growing Christians
- *Inspire holiness* in the lives of believers
- *Instill hope* in the hearts of struggling people everywhere

Because He's coming again!

Humor for a Teacher's Heart © 2004 by Howard Publishing Co., Inc.
All rights reserved. Printed in the United States of America
Published by Howard Publishing Co., Inc.
3117 North 7th Street, West Monroe, Louisiana 71291-2227
www.howardpublishing.com

05 06 07 08 09 10 11 12 13   10 9 8 7 6 5 4 3

Compiled by The Livingstone Corporation
Edited by Between the Lines
Cover art by Kristen Myers
Cover design by LinDee Loveland
Illustrated by Kristen Myers
Interior design by Tennille Paden

Library of Congress Cataloging-in-Publication Data

Humor for a teacher's heart : stories, quips, and quotes to lift the heart / compiled by the
   Livingstone Corporation ; illustrated b Kristen Myers.
      p. cm.
   ISBN 1-58229-394-5
   1. Teacher--Humor. 2. Christian education--Humor. I. Myers, Kristen. II. Livingstone
Corporation.

PN6231.S3H86 2004
371.02'02'07--dc22
                                                              2004047561

No part of this publication may be reproduced in any form without the prior written permission of the publisher except in the case of brief quotations within critical
articles and review.

Produced with the assistance of The Livingstone Corporation
(www.LivingstoneCorp.com). Project staff includes Joan Guest, Mary Horner
Collins, Mark Poole, Madison Trammel, and Ruth Lundgren.

Contents

Chapter 1: Starting Out

Chapter 2: Out of the Mouths of Babes

Chapter 3: Kindergarten Capers

Chapter 4: It's Elementary, My Dear

Chapter 5: Middle-School Madness

Chapter 6: High-School Happenings

Chapter 7: Stick to the Subject

Contents

Chapter 8: Those Amazing Subs

Chapter 9: Of Parents and Principals

Chapter 10: There Are Bad Days . . . and Then There's Teaching

Chapter 11: Beyond the Call of Duty

Chapter 12: Through a Student's Eyes

Chapter 13: This Is What It's All About

Source Notes—169

Contributors—175

Starting Out

S-E-X

LINDA STRATER

A college roommate of mine was doing her student teaching. While she watched the second graders practice their writing, a little boy raised his hand to get her attention. "Teacher, how do you spell sex?"

Startled at the question, my friend made her way to his desk and quietly asked, "What word did you want me to help you spell?"

The little boy replied, "I have the first part—I-N—but I don't know how to spell the whole word—Insects."

Confessions of a Student Teacher

Jeanne Zornes

Everything I needed to know in life, I learned as a student teacher of high-school English. Ten weeks of supervised apprenticeship left me mumbling, "To teach, or not to teach?" Part of my problem was being twenty-two and looking fifteen. I knew I was in trouble the day a teacher who hadn't seen me before inquired if I had a hall pass.

Worse, while I barely stretched out at five-foot-two, some of my students—thanks to testosterone in lethal combination with milk and pizza—loomed like Goliaths over me. I rationalized that they were specially bred for the school's championship football team, but I never got over being looked down on. What were they seeing? My cowlick? My dandruff?

Four years' distance from my own graduation had clouded my memories of true high-school life. I'll admit, I belonged to its cerebral clique that lived for SATs, physics, honors English, and

other tortures of secondary education. While our classmates did the weekly dances, we did Dante. While they checked out the newest steadies, we studied. So entering college was an easy transition for me. Each quarter's required reading for English majors nearly fried my eyes, but I dug in and did it. The symbolism in William Blake's poetry? No problem. A discussion of evil in *Macbeth*? Bring it on.

Then came my return to high school, to student teach one hundred and fifty teens in junior literature and oversee the newspaper staff. My college had specific goals for my "growth in essential teaching skills demonstrated in real classroom situations." My students rewrote the manual.

They had their own brand of psychology, translating Skinner's mazes into seventeen hundred sweaty bodies surging through skinny halls. They applied Pavlov's salivating dog experiments to the 11:27 lunch bell. They offered advice on curriculum: "If you want your future students to be happy, don't make them read *Our Town*." And on assignments: "Why do they have all those stupid hidden meanings in plays, stories, and poems?"

Under their tutelage, the college "Performance Profile of Basic Teaching Skills" came alive:

- *Developing objectives:* "Hey, Teach, are we going to do anything interesting today, or can I go to sleep?"

- *Controlling the interaction:* "Teacher, let's talk about Judy's broken foot instead of taking the spelling test."

- *Measuring results:* "My theme is all blurred and soggy because somebody stuffed my locker with snow."

- *Motivating low achievers:* "Hey, Teacher, ever had your tires slashed?"

Tomorrow, and tomorrow, and tomorrow crept in its petty pace—but finally the ten weeks ended. I managed a P for pass—and changed careers. My first job, after all those late-night cram sessions in Victorian literature, consisted of writing crime news and obituaries for a small-town newspaper. Then I was promoted to the Home Page, where I wrote headlines for recipes.

Eventually my career led me back to literature and writing articles, short stories, and books. But I never forgot my students' advice, such as this farewell note: "Don't grow old. You wouldn't look good in it."

Thirty-five years later I did grow old, and good or not, I look it. And I came back to the classroom part time, instructing adults instead of teens. The once baby-faced teacher who encountered high school's "double, double, toil and trouble" (thanks, weird sisters in *Macbeth*) now preaches, "What is this passive verb I see before me?"

And so far, nobody's threatened to slash my tires.

First Day of School
Teresa Bell Kindred

When I walked back into my old high school, I expected to feel as old and outdated as the bell-bottom jeans I had once worn. I was prepared for that; what I didn't expect was the smell. The building still smelled exactly as it did when I graduated back in 1974. It was an odd mix of antiseptic, dirty socks, and sweat, with a dash of pencil trimmings tossed in. Sniffing it didn't make me high or nauseated, just extremely nostalgic.

I didn't know an aroma could trigger so many memories. I had been so young and so sure of myself when I was a teenager, and totally worthless. In those days my only ambitions in life were to date a cute guy, graduate, and leave town—not necessarily in that order.

My eyes traveled the length of the gym across the honey-colored hardwood floors. The drapes that framed the stage were the same ones some of my more nervy classmates had used as a screen when

they wanted to make out between classes. I walked past the bleachers, where students were waiting for the first bell of the day. They hardly noticed me. How many times had my bony bottom sat on those painful wooden planks at ball games, pep rallies, or between classes? Hundreds, thousands? I hurried upstairs to the office. If I hesitated any longer, I might give up on the idea of teaching, skip the classroom, and go straight to the nursing home.

A dark-haired lady smiled at me from behind a desk. I tried to smile back, but I didn't have much control over my facial muscles. I was scared to death, and obviously it showed.

"Relax, honey. The kids here don't eat new teachers on their first day," she said with a smile. "They usually wait a week or so, then they roast them on the agriculture teacher's grill and eat them."

"Very funny," I said.

"My name's Peggy, and you can come to me if you need anything. The kids will tell you I'm just the secretary, but don't believe them. I really run this joint."

I liked her and later would learn she was telling the truth: she really did run the place.

"Thanks, Peggy. I'm looking for Mr. Tyler. Is he in his office?"

"Yes, he's expecting you. Be sure to knock loudly. If he's on the phone, he can't hear a thing in there. These block walls are ten inches thick."

I had to knock twice before he answered, and even then I wasn't sure what to do. It sounded like he said, "Come in," but his voice was so muffled I hesitated.

"I said come in!" Mr. Tyler bellowed from behind the door. "Ahh, Mrs. Kindred, are you ready for your first day?"

Mr. Tyler was what local people call a move-in. Neither he nor his parents or grandparents were born or raised in Metcalfe

 7

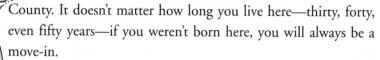

County. It doesn't matter how long you live here—thirty, forty, even fifty years—if you weren't born here, you will always be a move-in.

I nodded that I was ready, even though I wasn't. He came around the desk to escort me to my class. I followed him down the hall like an obedient puppy.

"I assume Dr. Fields told you that you'll be teaching the PALS program to students who are having trouble in their English classes," he said over his shoulder as he hurried along.

Dr. Fields was the superintendent and the person who had hired me. The teacher who ran the PALS lab had quit unexpectedly, leaving them in a bind. Dr. Fields had called the grocery store where I was working and asked if I was still interested in teaching. I assured him that I was, and that was all it took. I definitely wasn't the most experienced candidate for the job. All I knew about the program was that PALS stood for Principles of Adult Literacy. I only knew that because I'd called a friend and asked.

"Your classroom is in the back of the library. It's partitioned off from the rest of the room," he said as we walked through the library.

One look at the librarian's face, and I knew I was about as welcome in her library as a preacher in a house of ill repute.

"Good morning, Margaret," I said. She and I had graduated from high school together.

"Welcome," she said sternly. "Keep the noise down back there. I won't put up with foolishness."

Mr. Tyler ignored her and led me into the small room. I nodded and stepped inside. There wasn't even a door I could close. How in the world could I keep from disturbing her when we had

no door and were separated only by movable walls that left a foot of space at the top and bottom?

There were tables and computers, twelve in all. Computers. I knew even less about them than I did the PALS program. Bill, my husband, had just purchased one and tried to show me how to operate it, but I had declined, saying I had neither the time nor the interest to learn. How quickly things changed.

At the front of the room were a desk and a metal cabinet I assumed served as a storage area. My curiosity got the best of me and I tried to open the cabinet, but it was locked tight.

"They keep the rest of the equipment in there. I'll see if I can find a key for you," Mr. Tyler said.

More equipment? Was this a classroom or a locker room? Not wanting to seem as ignorant as I really was, I kept my mouth shut. Surely someone would tell me what to do sooner or later.

"Well, now that you're settled in, I have to get back to work," Mr. Tyler said. "Have a good day."

The bell rang, my heart sank, and he left. I stood for a moment staring at the computers. How in the world was I going to teach English to these kids with a program I knew absolutely nothing about, using computers I didn't even know how to turn on?

"Mrs. Kindred?"

I turned around. The lady in front of me was too old to be a student.

"Yes?"

"My name is Mallie Mason, and I'm your assistant," she said.

I didn't know whether to cry from relief or kiss her.

"Hallelujah," I said.

"Praise the Lord!" she replied instantly and raised her hands and face to the sky.

I had an assistant! A religious assistant! God hadn't forgotten me after all; surely Mallie Mason was heaven-sent.

The first bell was followed by the second, and my students were beginning to drift in. I picked up the class rosters from my desk.

"Miss Mason, there are only three classes listed here. Aren't there six periods a day?"

"Actually, there are eight," she replied.

"Eight! My word, how can there be eight?"

"Each class lasts forty to forty-five minutes. Lunch is twenty minutes, and break in the afternoon is eight to ten minutes."

I looked at her closely. She wasn't teasing. OK, eight classes. Well, the advantage would be that the day would pass quickly. I didn't want to think about the disadvantages.

"There's something strange about my classes," I said as I scanned the list of names. "All my students are boys."

Miss Mason nodded. "That's right."

"You the new teacher?" a tall, skinny young man with tobacco-stained teeth asked, right before he spat a wad of something in the general direction of my trash can.

I thought about correcting his grammar, but that seemed pointless at the moment. I considered telling him tobacco products weren't allowed at school, but that didn't seem like a good idea either. By now several boys had filtered in, and they were all staring at me, waiting to see what I would do. I decided to ignore

what had just happened and deal with it after class, providing I lived that long.

"Yes, I'm the new teacher. My name is Mrs. Kindred."

"Kinerd, what kind of name is that?"

"Not Kinerd, Kindred."

"I got an uncle in the state pen, his last name's Kinnard. You any kin to him?"

"No, I don't think so."

I looked at Miss Mason for a clue as to what would come next. "Don't ask him why he's in the pen," she whispered.

That was the last thing on my mind.

"OK, let's all take a seat, and then I'll call roll."

A boy with long, scraggly hair—neither blond nor brown, just the color of dirty—burst into the room and with a leap managed to land right at my feet on his behind.

"You said take a seat!" he said loudly. "This here's the one I want!"

All the boys heehawed hysterically.

I looked at my watch. Only three more hours and my first day would be over.

Would I make it? Would I come back tomorrow? I didn't know. But I knew one thing for sure: if I did come back, it would be with a spare bottle of Tylenol.

Meet the Teacher

Joni Woodward

"Hello, I'm happy to meet you. I've been enjoying having your child in my class."

This was the little speech I had memorized in honor of my first Meet-the-Teacher Night. It was my only ammunition in a sparse arsenal of positive comments. I hid my terror behind bright eyes and an enthusiastic smile. Excessive energy propelled me from one handshake to another as I met the parents of my first graders. Their names left my brain as soon as their faces left my sight.

I could hardly believe it had been three weeks since school started. My life had been a flurry of activity. I had graduated that August on a Friday and started teaching the next Monday. Plucked from my life as a student, I was now firmly planted in the life of a teacher. It was sink or swim, and by now I was mentally sinking.

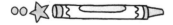 

As another stranger approached me, I felt a sudden separation from my body. It seemed as though I were on the ceiling looking down at a face that fully expected to be recognized. He shook my hand, oblivious to my distress.

"I've been wanting to meet you personally for a long time," he said jovially. "Did you know I'm an acquaintance of your uncle's? I see him up in Austin several times a year."

I racked my brain. *OK, he knows my Uncle Red who lives five hours away.* Did I recall my uncle mentioning he knew someone in my school district? No, I did not.

"I know he's proud of you," the man continued. "Tell him I said hello the next time you talk to him."

Kind eyes stared into mine. I couldn't let him leave without knowing his name. If he was a parent, I'd be seeing him throughout the year. The subject of my uncle was bound to come up again.

I gave up the pretense. "And you are?" I prodded.

His smile dropped immediately. "I'm Rudy Haggard," he answered gruffly.

I stood stiff with embarrassment as I watched my assistant superintendent walk out of my classroom.

Out of the Mouths
of Babes

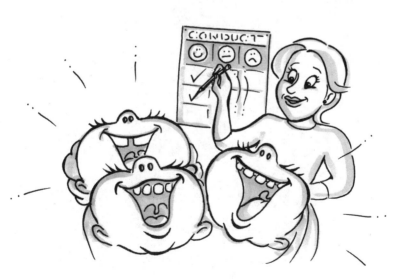

Mrs. Teacher
MARY ANN BERTRAM

My daughter introduced me to a little girl who was new to the neighborhood. "This is my mom, Mrs. Bertram."

The new girl looked at me and said, "You must be a teacher."

I was surprised and said, "Yes, I am. How did you know?"

The little girl answered, "Because your first name is Mrs."

Jesus, Kids, and Me

Dena Dyer

Jesus called his followers "little children." The Gospels show him as a man who loved kids and loved to teach. He even loved to teach kids. What a guy! When I instruct children, my back tightens, my eyes narrow, and my head starts to spin. It's like *Mister Rogers* meets *The Exorcist*. Not a pretty sight.

The funny thing is, I love to teach adults and teenagers. They're clean, quiet, and interested in the lesson. Especially when I bring doughnuts.

Still, God has used my experiences with kids to make me aware of my less attractive qualities. I really try to relax when I help at my son's school or go to a birthday party. I hug the kids, ask them questions, and listen to them. And I have a notebook handy for all the funny and amazing things they say.

Once during a stint leading children's theater classes, I taught a six-year-old cutie with red curls, sparkling eyes, and a mischievous

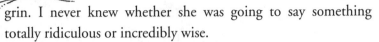

grin. I never knew whether she was going to say something totally ridiculous or incredibly wise.

During one session, as I was auditioning the children for speaking parts in our year-end production, I noticed Ann pounding her head with her notebook.

"Ann!" I exclaimed. "What in the world are you doing?"

"Hitting myself on the head," she said.

"I can see that, but why are you doing it?" I asked.

"My finger hurts, and this makes me forget about it."

Another golden moment came when I volunteered to help with the four- and five-year-olds at our church. The nursery was overrun with kids, and the workers desperately needed help. (Later I found out why. Teaching Sunday school is like being sent to Alcatraz—once you go in, you don't come out.)

But as a minister's wife, I thought I would set a good example for the other adults and help with the pre-K class for a while. As it turned out, I nearly ruined my witness during my three-month tenure.

The children were cute, but they never listened. I wasn't a parent then, or I wouldn't have taken it so personally. Also, some of the kids seemed to be going for the Oldest Child Still in Diapers entry in the *Guinness Book of World Records*.

Another Sunday, Katie interrupted the Bible story with something "very important" she needed to tell the class. I decided to let her speak, thinking she'd been overcome by a spiritual revelation (brought on by my excellent teaching, of course).

"What is it, sweetheart?" I asked.

"Happy Birthday, Elvis!" she yelled.

I think that was my last Sunday.

Yes, the Gospels often show Jesus inviting the children to come to him. Can't you see him—like some cuddly, magnetic junglegym—laughing as the moppets climb all over him? Thankfully, God has worked on me when it comes to kids. (Having one will do that to you.) In fact, I'm actually volunteering to help in Vacation Bible School at our church this year. No teaching involved, just assisting. After all, it's only five days . . . Oh Lord, what have I done?

Grandma's Creation

Gary Crandall

Lindsey was a four-year-old girl in my wife's Sunday school class. At the end of the lesson on Creation, my wife, Sherrie, asked, "Who made the earth?"

"God," a chorus of voices replied.

"And who made the sun?" Sherrie prompted.

The reply was unanimous. "God!"

"And who made the stars?"

Everyone responded with "God"—except for Lindsey. At the top of her voice, she said, "Grandma!"

When Sherrie ran through the questions again, once again Lindsey insisted that it was her grandma who made the stars, not God.

Not long after, Sherrie saw Lindsey's grandmother and mentioned the curious exchange. The first words out of her mouth were, "Well, my stars!"

 20

Look Who's Watching
Linda Gilden

Jon and Brad sat on the red carpet. Brad was surrounded by blocks. Jon was off to one side, leaning toward Brad's construction project with obvious curiosity. There were plenty of blocks for everyone in the class of four-year-olds, but today these two boys wanted to play with the same ones.

"Brad, you know you need to share the blocks," Jon said, echoing the tone I had used many times with his classmates. Brad's house was almost as tall as he was, but he didn't show much interest in sharing the blocks he had left.

"I'm building a 'partment. It's gonna be big, and I need all the blocks," Brad quickly told Jon. He began to pull the extra pieces closer to him.

"I'll help you then," Jon offered. "We can make it really big." He stretched his short arms as far out as he could for emphasis, then reached for a block.

"No, this is *my* 'partment. You can build your own later, when it's your turn."

But Jon wasn't giving up. "Brad, you need to give me a turn. We need to share with our friends. After all, you know who's watching."

My teacher's pride began to swell. The unit we had just finished included a section on how it pleased God when we're nice to our friends. I had particularly emphasized the concept of sharing, knowing it wasn't something four-year-olds do well.

And now this darling little boy was demonstrating that he had grasped the concept. It's every teacher's dream—to see the lessons taught become part of the lives of her students.

Brad looked around the room and then back at Jon with a blank stare. "Who's watching?"

"Santa Claus. He watches all year to see if we're being good."

Hark! The Herald Preschoolers Sing
(with Apologies to Luke Chapter Two)
Bob Welch

[1]And it came to pass, that there went out a decree from my son's preschool, that all teachers should be taxed to their emotional limits by having their students put on Christmas programs.

[2](And this decree was first made when Virginia Sokol was teaching my son's class at Highland Christian School.)

[3]And all went to the stage to practice, everyone in his own little world, including Joseph, who wore red high tops and a semipunk hairdo.

[4]And I also went unto the school, in the city of Bellevue, Washington, for I had vowed to watch these rehearsals and the final performance, even if holiday traffic was the pits.

[5]And with Mrs. Sokol were two assistants, who were great with patience, even during the first rehearsal, when in the middle of "Away in a Manger," an angel said unto them, "Teacher, I'm tired of standing."

⁶And so it was that, while these four-year-olds were there, Mrs. Sokol brought forth the script for the program in the fellowship hall because there was no room for the program in their classroom, being as they had recently packed Christmas presents for their parents using millions of those white polystyrene plastic chips and the place looked like a scene from the movie *Avalanche*.

⁷And there were in the same fellowship hall shepherds abiding on the stage, keeping watch over their jingle bells, because they were to be used later in the program. And for four-year-old shepherds, jingle bells are infinitely more fun than wooden staffs because they make noise, and to misplace them is a major bummer.

⁸Besides the shepherds, also abiding were Adam and Eve, Noah, and three sets of animals from the ark; this was no ordinary Christmas program, you see, but more of a Cliffs Notes of biblical history.

⁹And lo, the first rehearsal came upon them and I was sore afraid because (a) there was a near riot when the jingle bells were passed out (everyone wanted blue); (b) Noah and Eve were flirting, which wasn't going over big with Adam; and (c) Joseph was so in tune to this historical reenactment that he spent most of the time stretching his lower lip forward with both hands in the apparent attempt to make a suitable landing pad for a small helicopter.

¹⁰And as the rehearsals continued, one of the angels started to take off his rugby shirt, and Noah got his hand stuck in his pocket, and the ark nearly capsized, and Joseph missed a practice because of the flu.

¹¹And Mrs. Sokol said unto me, "Fear not, for behold, I bring you good tidings of great joy. For unto you this day, in the city of

Bellevue, has been given one of the smoother practices, based on fiascos we've had in the past, like the time two staff-wielding shepherds tried to re-create the Luke Skywalker–Darth Vader battle scene."

[12]But, verily, she reminded me, the children before you have their hearts in the right place, even if one of the rabbits from the ark occasionally gets mixed in with the three kings.

[13]And seeing the wonder of the rehearsals, I figured this shall be a sign unto the parents that the final performance is going well: Ye shall find your babes wrapped in bathrobes and standing on the stage, none of them picking their noses and each of their zippers up.

[14]And suddenly there was a multitude of nervous parents and teachers flitting around as if backstage before a Broadway performance of *Hello, Dolly!* and a multitude of angels and shepherds and kings saying, "Teacher, I have to go to the bathroom." And lo, I knew it was showtime.

[15]And it came to pass, as the parents exited backstage to be seated and focus their camcorders, that Adam, in so many words, said that it was going to take more than the lure of an apple to get him out on that stage. And he wept.

[16]And lo, a voice from afar comforted him, saying, "Hey, nifty outfit; not even the real Adam had thongs."

[17]And another voice, this one from a panicked mother who had arrived with her plain-clothed child, came down from above, saying, "Oh no, the kids weren't supposed to come in costumes today, were they?"

[18]And then Noah spake, saying, "Aren't I supposed to have a mustache and beard or something?"

[19]Then Mrs. Sokol beckoned the children, saying, "Let us

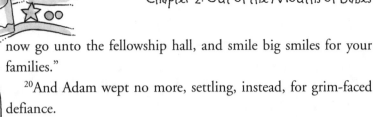

now go unto the fellowship hall, and smile big smiles for your families."

[20]And Adam wept no more, settling, instead, for grim-faced defiance.

[21]And when they had come to the place beneath the star and stood each on his piece of masking tape, Mrs. Sokol rejoiced with exceeding great joy, as if she had just led a party of climbers to the top of Mount Everest, and said to the audience, "You don't realize this, but you have just witnessed a miracle."

[22]And those who had come unto the stage found the babe in the manger with Mary, who looked as if she would rather be anywhere else than in this manger—say, doing wind sprints in Death Valley in late August.

[23]Meanwhile Joseph was delayed, having tripped on his shoelaces and fallen flat on his face while going up the steps.

[24]And they brought forth a gift, a birthday cake with three candles, which Mary blew out in only three puffs.

[25]And they sang, each in his own key, a multitude of songs, including "Happy Birthday to You" to Jesus.

[26]And suddenly a sound of great joy resounded from on high. For the audience was fervently clapping, having realized that their children—in all their innocence and imperfection—had proclaimed to the world the perfect Christmas message: Glory to God in the highest, and on earth peace, good will toward men.

[27]And lo, at least one parent felt a lump in his throat and asked himself: When was the last time I did as much?

Preschool Germs

Cindy Thomson

I have spent many years as a preschool teacher in a church setting. Every day spent with three- and four-year-olds is filled with smiles, chuckles, or bouts of uncontrollable laughter. Young children are incredibly honest and observant, and what matters to adults is often of no consequence to them.

One day at snack time, we let the children help themselves, family style. On a long rectangular table, we placed baskets of crackers, apple slices, carrots, and small cookies. In the center we placed a small plastic juice pitcher with a wide spout—just right for tiny hands to maneuver. While this helped to foster independence and motor skills, it also sometimes proved to be a hygiene and sanitation problem.

One girl at the table (I'll call her Julie) never seemed concerned about hand washing, the proper use of facial tissues, covering her mouth when she coughed, and other matters of

 27

personal hygiene. So on this particular day as we sat at the snack table, I coached the kids.

"Before we begin," I said, "I want to tell you all something." I had observed children the previous day trying to grab the pitcher by the spout. "If you put your fingers on this part," I explained while carefully pointing to the spout, "you'll pass your germs on to the next person who pours the juice."

Feeling satisfied that I'd done a good job explaining proper table manners, I added, "Now does anyone need anything?" Eight cherubic faces glowed back at me. Some nodded, some smiled, and others rolled their eyes, obviously wishing I'd let them eat. Julie sat next to me and raised her hand.

"Mrs. Thomson?"

"Yes, Julie?" I thought I had finally reached her. She'd probably never wipe her nose with her hands again!

"I need something," Julie said, straightening herself in her pint-sized chair.

"What do you need, sweetheart?"

She pointed at the juice pitcher. "Please pass the germs!"

Kindergarten Capers

No Cheating!

MARGO TAYLOR

My five-year-old grandson, Tyler, was looking forward to starting kindergarten until he saw a video in which a young boy was caught and punished for cheating. For several days, Tyler voiced his concern about going to school.

The day before he started kindergarten, Tyler ran to his mother, excited and quite pleased. "Mommy, it's OK. I know I can't cheat!" he exclaimed. "I can't cheat because I don't know how to write!"

Give Your Best

Linda Gilden

My kindergarten class filed onto the stage, which was decorated to perfection. The homemade ornaments adorning the tree added a special touch.

This was the day we had all waited and practiced for. The children bounced with excitement, every boy and girl dressed in his or her Christmas best. The stage was a mass of red, white, and green, of smiles and wiggles.

The program progressed smoothly. I smiled at the children, and they smiled back. They seemed to remember every instruction I had given them before they left the classroom. This was my first year teaching music at the weekday preschool, and I wanted everything to be just right.

Mamie started her solo, her sweet voice filling the room. She looked like an angel. I glanced at the audience. Many were nodding and smiling. One dear lady wiped a tear.

Finally I began to relax and enjoy the presentation.

At just the right moment, the wise men came down the aisle. They walked slowly, counting to three between each step, just as we had practiced. They held their gifts level with their belly buttons, another of their preperformance instructions. I saw the lead wise man grin as he passed his mother.

Chris was one of the last children to speak. He stepped proudly to the microphone, took a deep breath, and began.

"The wise men brought their best gifts to Jesus. They brought gold, Frankenstein, and Smurfs."

Chris got quite an ovation. He lingered for a moment behind the microphone, chest thrust out, all smiles. He had done his best.

That's all any of us can do. God gave his very best gift to us. When we bring our gifts to Jesus, they don't have to be perfect. They just need to be our best, given from hearts of love.

Undies

Amy Jenkins

My son D. J.'s kindergarten teacher was creatively teaching her class the alphabet by designating a letter for each day. Each student would bring an item that started with this letter. On previous alphabet days, we'd tried to be original—a crucible for C and llama pictures for L. But we were stumped when it came to U.

D. J. and I finally decided on an umbrella. What I didn't know was that D. J. and my husband had put their heads together too and packed underwear. Later that day, my husband told me what he did.

"That's going to embarrass D. J.," I said. "The other kids will make fun of him."

I knew I was right when my son, pouting, got in the car after school. Head down, he said, "Mom, how could you do that to me? I was so embarrassed. All the kids brought umbrellas."

Then he brightened. "At least I was the only one with underwear."

The Calm before the Storm
Mary Horner Collins

I spent a wonderful and challenging year in South America teaching kindergarten and music in a missionary school. As the sweet little five-year-olds gathered the first day on the rug, I anticipated a fun year of playing and learning together. But I hadn't anticipated David.

David was what I like to call energetic. You know, like a tornado is energetic or like an eighteen wheeler is energetic. He twirled and roared around the room, knocking over blocks, toppling toys to the floor, scattering papers helter-skelter, hurling crayons, and always talking. David was my little chatterbox, offering running commentary about most anything. Any question I asked the class, David would yell out an answer. If I needed a volunteer, David would raise his hand, but always with vocal accompaniment.

David was never still and never at a loss for words. But often I was. This was my first year of teaching, and sometimes I didn't quite know what to do with all the five-year-old bundles of energy in my class. Along with teaching the ABCs and how to read, I spent many moments trying to teach David (and all the other children) classroom etiquette—to raise his hand first, to let others speak, to sit still, to work quietly, and to be considerate.

So one day I was quite pleased to see David sitting quietly at the table doing his paperwork. He seemed to have learned to control his energy and wasn't talking out loud or touching the other children. *Well, finally,* I thought, *something I've taught is getting through to him.* It was such a joy to see a child respond and learn to behave.

Then without warning, David threw up all over the table. So much for etiquette.

As we cleaned him up and called his mother to come get him, I had to laugh. The flu—not my wonderful influence—had brought on David's good behavior. But we all hoped he'd feel better soon. It was just a little too quiet in our classroom without him.

What Do You Want to Be?

James McCullen

I was invited by my daughter to attend open house at the elementary school, where I could view the classroom and work done by my grandchild Brandon and other kindergartners.

I arrived late. The room was empty, with the exception of Brandon's teacher. I walked in and introduced myself. Mrs. Caldwell said that she was happy to meet me and that I had made a good impression on my grandson. That made this papa's chest swell, as I'm quite proud of Brandon.

Mrs. Caldwell then told of the time she had asked all of her kindergartners what they wanted to be when they grew up. Brandon had said he wanted to be a preacher like his papa.

I bragged that when Brandon was three years old, he would stand behind the pulpit of the church I pastored and hold the microphone. All the family would sit and listen to him "preach." He would point his finger at "his congregation" and say,

 36

"Zacchaeus, you come down, for I'm going to your house today."
I explained that this was from a Bible story Brandon had learned
in Sunday school.

Mrs. Caldwell laughed and said, "Well, you can be very proud
of him. He's a smart little boy."

When I returned home, Brandon was busy playing with his
favorite toys, Teenage Mutant Ninja Turtle figures. I didn't want
to embarrass him, so I took him aside and, in a boastful tone,
told him what Mrs. Caldwell had said about his future aspira-
tions.

My pride was quickly deflated, however, when Brandon
replied, "I told her that because I didn't think she knew what a
Ninja Turtle was. When I get big, I really want to be a Ninja
Turtle."

Holy Moses

Sharon Hinck

The church was desperate for Sunday school teachers. That must have been the rationale of the education committee. Though I was an inexperienced high-school sophomore, when I volunteered to teach, they gave me a class of my own.

If they had known about my flair for the dramatic, they might have given it more thought.

Using bedsheets, I transformed my kindergarten classroom into a fort and created secret entrances. Each week I tried to outdo myself with more exciting ways to share Bible stories with the children. The superintendent was kind enough to provide us with flannelboard images to use in telling the stories, but somehow those didn't do enough to capture the pathos and spectacle of the lesson each week.

So I recruited Ted.

Ted was a friend from my high school. Easygoing, a good

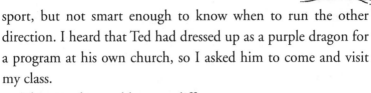

sport, but not smart enough to know when to run the other direction. I heard that Ted had dressed up as a purple dragon for a program at his own church, so I asked him to come and visit my class.

This time he would wear a different costume.

I was teaching about Moses. The students made Popsicle-stick baskets to float in the bulrushes and created vivid finger paintings of the plagues in Egypt. But as we neared the end of the unit, I believed they deserved something special: a visit from the hero himself.

Enter Ted—complete with patriarchal beard, imposing staff, and a dusty tunic that looked suspiciously like someone's old bedspread.

"My camel is waiting outside in the parking lot."

The children were enthralled. Ted's impersonation was just the right blend of Santa Claus and Charlton Heston. He asked the children questions about the Bible stories they had learned, and they answered, round-eyed and awestruck—even when Ted forgot his role and slipped into an occasional "Ho, ho, ho."

All too soon the hour had passed.

"Sorry, kids. Time for me to leave."

"But how will you get back to Egypt?" one eager five-year-old asked.

"My camel is waiting outside in the parking lot," Ted said with all the grave authority of Moses.

He left amid shouted thanks and happy waves.

Neither of us realized the riot that would occur in the church

parking lot as a dozen manic kindergartners dragged their parents outside to find the camel Moses had told them would be there.

Ted ditched the bedspread and beard, and we blended into the crowd, watching the chaos.

"Really, Mommy!" we heard one little girl wail as she tugged her mom's hand. "There's a camel in the parking lot. Moses told us so!" I had the feeling I'd have some explaining to do to the education committee.

I smiled at Ted. "So next month we're studying Joseph. Wanna come back?"

Ted looked at me with a hint of panic. Turns out he had learned something that day too: how to run.

It's Elementary, My Dear

Sad Face
Jo Ann Cook

I was trying to impress upon my first-grade Sunday school class the importance of individually receiving God's gift of salvation. I thought a simple illustration might be helpful. "What do you do when someone gives you a birthday present?" I asked.

One little girl was quick to answer: "You say thank you—unless it's clothes. Then you put a really sad look on your face."

Do You Live Here?

Kari Ziman

The observations and mental processes of a five-year-old mind are amazing. A few months into teaching first grade, I was sitting at my desk before school began, preparing for the day. One of my students, Jason, unexpectedly ran into the room. He put his backpack on his desk and turned to his father, who stood in the doorway.

"Come on, Dad!" he said. "Mrs. Ziman is here! See—here in the classroom where I go to school!" Wide-eyed and with a huge grin on his face, he exclaimed, "But Mrs. Ziman, what are you doing here already?" Laughing, I told him I was getting ready to teach him for the day.

"Does it take a long time?" he asked.

"Just a little bit of work before school, after school, and some-times even on the weekends," I replied. "But Jason, I love getting ready to teach you and the rest of the class."

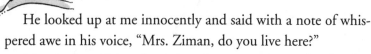

He looked up at me innocently and said with a note of whispered awe in his voice, "Mrs. Ziman, do you live here?"

I laughed, realizing that when Jason goes home for the day, I'm at school, and when he arrives, I'm at school.

"Jason, if I live here, where is my bed?"

Jason slowly looked around, as if he had never seen the room before in his life. A look of acknowledgment spread across his face. "Ahh, Mrs. Ziman, you couldn't live here. Where would you hang your clothes?"

"True, but I could hang them on the flagpole by the blackboard. Have you ever seen my clothes in here? The bigger problem as I see it, Jason, is where would I take a shower?"

He giggled and looked up at his dad. With an all-knowing tone of voice, Jason said, "Dad, they don't have showers at school. I know because I've checked."

I laughed, gave Jason a hug, and sent him out to the playground.

How to Destroy Graven Images

Silvana Clark

I know how to sell myself at job interviews. Walk right in, give a firm handshake, and then dazzle the interviewer with my wit and confidence. Studies say the decision to hire someone is made within the first thirty seconds. People have offered me jobs within twenty-five seconds because I know how to make a great first impression. Here's the catch: I get hired for jobs that are way above my skill level. Impressed with my interview skills, people offer me jobs better suited for someone with, say, experience and relevant skills.

So there I was, the children's director of a large church. The hiring committee overlooked the fact that I was a new Christian, had never attended Sunday school, and certainly had no idea how to teach children. But I sure knew how to conduct myself at a job interview! My first assignment involved teaching a third-grade Sunday school class until their regular teacher returned

45

from a lengthy vacation. Glancing through the curriculum, I noticed they were studying the Ten Commandments. "Thou shalt have no graven images" caught my attention.

On Sunday morning my new students walked into their classroom to find it a veritable building center for graven images.

Who had time for a meaningful lesson when there were graven images to construct?

"We're going to build graven images!" I announced in the same enthusiastic voice I used during my job interview.

The eight-year-olds had no clue what a graven image was, but they eagerly set out constructing things with toilet-paper rolls and empty boxes. Rolls of duct tape helped to hold five-foot-high cardboard structures together. Giant plastic wiggle eyes added intriguing features to idols made from beach balls and empty milk jugs. Kids had paint on their clothes and smiles on their faces. Sunday school had never been like this! The room could pass as a warehouse for graven images. I never bothered to explain the relationship to the Ten Commandments or to any form of biblical application. Who had time for a meaningful lesson when there were graven images to construct? The class worked cheerfully for a full hour.

Suddenly I noticed parents were arriving to pick up their children. I knew I had to get some sort of message across to the students.

"Listen carefully," I said. "The Bible says we shouldn't worship any graven images."

They looked at me with wide eyes.

"So, let's destroy all these statues!"

With that, all of us—fifteen kids and myself—began ripping apart the graven images. Boxes flew through the air, beachballs got smashed, and boxes covered in wet paint ended up staining the carpet. Parents walked in to a frenzy of wild, yelling kids.

"Destroy, destroy!" The children stomped on the graven images.

One father was hit in the head with a wiggle-eyed milk jug. Another girl began crying because she wanted to take her graven image home. Parents with stunned faces grabbed their children and swept them away to safety.

That's one Sunday school lesson none of us will ever forget!

The Skinny on Ants

Amy Jenkins

My eight-year-old daughter Sally was proudly explaining her science lesson to me. She learned that herbivores are plant eaters and carnivores are meat eaters.

I decided to test her knowledge by naming an animal and having her classify it.

"Tiger."

"Carnivore."

"Rabbit."

"Herbivore."

"Anteater."

"Herbivore."

"An anteater's a herbivore?" I asked. "Don't they eat ants? Wouldn't that make them carnivores?"

In an instant, Sally had it figured out. "There's not much meat on an ant."

Spare Sodom?
Lois Bergy

One Sunday I was teaching my junior-church kids, ages seven through twelve, the story of Abraham pleading with the Lord not to destroy Sodom and the righteous people living there. I explained how Abraham started by asking that the city be spared if there were fifty righteous folks there, then forty-five, then thirty, then twenty.

I continued, "Finally, Abraham asked that Sodom be spared if there were only ten who loved the Lord there. And what do you think God said?"

I paused.

One little boy raised his hand and said, "I think God said, 'Don't push your luck!'"

Liar, Liar

Len Woods

Our church had a mini missions conference for children, to teach about the unreached peoples of the world. The guest speaker, a missionary, spoke passionately of the great spiritual needs in China.

"Now children," she said, "there are millions and millions of boys and girls in China who need to know that Jesus loves them and that he died for them so they can live in heaven forever. But you know what? The government in China doesn't want missionaries to come to China. They don't want their people to believe in Jesus. So when they catch someone telling others about the Bible, do you know what they do? They put them in jail and treat them terribly."

The guest speaker continued enthusiastically. "And so, boys and girls, if I want to go to China and tell others about Jesus, what do I have to be?"

From the back of the room, one little boy yelled out, "A liar?"

Middle-School
Madness

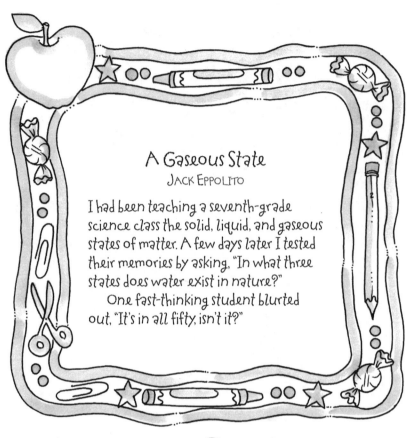

A Gaseous State
JACK EPPOLITO

I had been teaching a seventh-grade science class the solid, liquid, and gaseous states of matter. A few days later I tested their memories by asking, "In what three states does water exist in nature?"

One fast-thinking student blurted out, "It's in all fifty, isn't it?"

That Old Sew-and-Sew

Marilyn Meberg

When I was in seventh grade, I had an experience in my sewing class that, if I had been evaluated on the basis of my performance, would have scored me a zero! I had come into the class optimistically expecting to master the art of sewing within the first few weeks. My confidence was reinforced by the teacher's promise that we could all become expert seamstresses by the end of the semester.

The first week of class was entitled "Knowing Our Machine." I soon discovered my machine had no desire to be known. In fact, it had no interest in a relationship whatsoever! I watched intently as our teacher demonstrated the intricate maze the thread had to follow from the spool to the needle. Every time I thought I had successfully completed each step and pressed the lever to begin the magical process of sewing, the thread would be

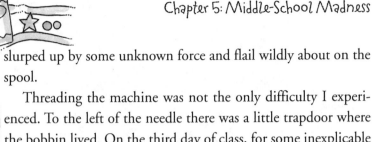

slurped up by some unknown force and flail wildly about on the spool.

Threading the machine was not the only difficulty I experienced. To the left of the needle there was a little trapdoor where the bobbin lived. On the third day of class, for some inexplicable reason, my bobbin chose to fling itself out upon the floor and go racing across the room. The thread was bright red and left a telltale path to my machine.

At this point my classmates gleefully assumed my ineptitude would provide them innumerable laughs throughout the semester. The teacher, however, did not appear to relish that prospect. She loomed over my machine with errant bobbin in hand and spoke in carefully controlled tones, "Apparently we don't know our machine."

The project for the class was to make a pair of pajamas. I chose a flannel fabric with little pink rosebuds. I soon found out that repeated ripping and sewing causes the threads in the fabric to separate and the design to become indistinguishable. It soon became impossible to discern if there were rosebuds, windmills, or frogs in the design.

As the semester progressed, and I did not, I was in serious danger of failing. I was horrified—I had never failed a class before. I needed much more help than I felt free to ask for. By now the teacher had adopted a certain stance toward me that was very disconcerting. She had the most peculiar response anytime she saw me heading toward her desk with my fragile pajamas extended before me. She would begin to take in air, and the longer I remained at her desk the more air she took in. There were times when I was sure the teacher doubled in size. Not only was I inhibited by this response, I was also unable to understand

what she said as the sucked-in air whistled slightly through her clenched teeth. I usually fled from her desk in defeat and relief, and the audible expulsion of her breath signaled that she had once again survived her massive inhalations.

The day before the class was over, I was still working to finish my pajamas. Shortly before the bell rang, I triumphantly put in the final stitch. I gingerly took the pajamas up to the teacher for her final inspection. To my dismay, through clenched teeth, she ordered, "Try them on."

I did not think the fabric could withstand the pressure of my body. The teacher was adamant, however, so I complied. I could not believe my eyes. I had sewn the left leg into the right arm and the right arm into the left leg. I tried every possible way to scrunch up my body so that maybe I could get by with them as they were, but I would have had to be deformed in order to pass them off as a good fit.

My friend Jane, when she recovered from hysterics, promised to help me take out each wrong stitch with a straight pin after school and then pin the leg and the arm into their proper places. All I needed to do the next day was put in the final stitches. It seemed simple enough.

The next day I settled down with my machine and began to sew very carefully. Within twenty minutes I had finished. I leaped jubilantly to my feet with the intention of rushing up to my teacher to show her my completed project. In my haste, I neglected to pull the lever up to release the needle from the cloth. My sudden movement knocked the machine off balance. As I stepped back from the falling machine, I realized I had inadvertently sewn my skirt into the pajama top so that I could not free myself from the material or from the fall. I flew over the top of

the machine and lay sprawled on the floor in final surrender to a machine that had sought to defeat me all semester.

My friends shrieked in hysterics.

For once the teacher did not begin her usual inhalations; she merely put her head down on her desk.

Finally Jane cut me loose with giant pinking shears.

I soon began to laugh about my experience.

My dad told me some weeks after the class was over that although he and Mom felt sorry for me as I muddled my way through sewing, they also had to exercise tremendous self-control when I told them of my hard-to-believe errors. On several occasions they laughed uncontrollably when they were alone.

Mom told me that she had never been able to grasp the details of sewing, had absolutely abhorred the class she had to take in high school, and hoped never to see a sewing machine again. We began to laugh about incidents from our respective classes, until finally, it became a family joke to request a sewing machine for Christmas each year.

Even now, one of my dad's favorite lines is to admire something I'm wearing and then in mock seriousness ask, "Did you make that yourself?"

Redhead Prejudice

Bianca Elliott

I feel passionately against any and all forms of prejudice and try to fight it when I can. I thought I was reasonably free from it until one of my classes in college revealed a chink in my armor. I did have a prejudice against redheads. I dealt with it the best I could as I went into teaching. Little did I know how this bias would flare up when I tried to be vulnerable and teach a group of students about prejudice.

The first time was in middle school. Not only were there red-heads in the class, there were many of them—too many. I tried to breathe and stay calm, but every day they acted like redheads. You know, coy, cute, annoying, ditsy, saucy, stubborn, and so on. They were really getting on my nerves. Then came the lesson on prejudice.

One of my goals as a teacher is to make the material real to the students. I like it when students ask, "When am I ever going

 57

to use this?" So I wanted this lesson to go from the superficial "We shouldn't hate others" to the real "What is your personal prejudice?"—and then to deal with it.

Have you ever said or done something that made sense to you but was horribly misunderstood by others? Well, we started off harmlessly enough, identifying where some prejudices start—parents and television—and listing them on the board. Then it got quiet. Now was the time to move and be vulnerable.

I told the class about my early life living in trailer courts and on welfare, about which I suffered much prejudice. I even related how I was the minority once in a school and how that felt. Then I moved on to how even little things can become a prejudice, like my annoyance with redheads. It got quiet again.

Oops. Oh, well, the lesson was taught. I redid the lesson the next year and filed it away under "good intentions."

Soon I moved to teaching high school and was enjoying it immensely. One day the school magazine had an article by a student named Lauren, who had been in my class at the middle school. I didn't start sweating until I read the title, which included "redheads."

Sure enough, Lauren shared her feelings about being a redhead. She had beautiful, long, red hair and freckles. She waited until the second paragraph to get me. Somehow, over the years, my brief sharing of a simple little prejudice became—in print— "Mrs. Elliott said, 'I hate redheads!'"

I read on, mortified. Later I spoke with Lauren, and she assured me she was only making a point in her article. Actually it was a point similar to the one I had made, so there were no hard feelings. She too hated prejudice. And I discovered I really do like redheads after all.

The Whichit

Deedee Muehlbauer

Once students walk into the classroom, the day has begun for every teacher. For the organized educator, it can be a calm, peaceful event. But as someone who's not a morning person and has to have coffee coursing through her veins before anyone can speak, it was always a frantic time for me. My desk was never organized, and I always felt like I was two steps behind as homeroom began. Once my students got to know me, they understood it was best to leave me alone until first period. For me to give an intelligent answer before then was always a challenge.

As I stood in my classroom with the familiar sounds of slamming lockers and laughing teenagers, just like every other day, the eighth graders came plodding in laden with books, and I finished my last sip of coffee. Some students laughed, some talked, and others looked like they just woke up. Then, like clockwork,

at 8:20 the school day began with the Pledge of Allegiance and a moment of silence.

Every morning, as the last word of the Pledge was uttered, I would plunge into my normal routine of attendance, lunch count, and getting together whatever final items were necessary to begin my first class. One day, as my head was down and I was flipping through the colossal mess that lived on my desk, one of my favorite students came up to me.

"Mrs. M?" she asked as I shuffled papers around.

"Yes, Dawn," I answered, barely knowing she was there.

"I have a question for you," she said.

"Sure, what is it?" I asked, looking for something I'm sure was terribly important at the moment.

She stood at my desk, hesitating for a moment. "What does *whichit* mean?"

As her question began to register in my head, I stopped plundering my desk and looked at her. "*Whichit*? What do you mean, Dawn?" It sounded like she was asking me about some type of tool.

"You know," she explained, "'for whichit stands.'"

For a moment I just looked at her, waiting for the caffeine to jolt my brain.

"Oh," I chuckled to myself when it finally hit me. "Dawn, *which* and *it* are two separate words. 'For . . . which . . . it . . . stands.'"

"Oh!" she exclaimed as I saw the light bulb go on in her head.

For a moment I just looked at her, waiting for the caffeine to jolt my brain.

As she walked back to her desk, I wondered how many other students were confused by common phrases we use every day. I can't correct all the misunderstandings, but I felt good that on this particular day, I had fixed one. I knew at least one student wouldn't grow up thinking our nation was propped up on a whichit.

Opera
Jennifer Blaske

"When I heard we'd be learning about opera, I thought this was going to be the worst six weeks of my life."

I was used to this sort of reaction from my seventh-grade music students. On the first day of class, when I explained to them that we would be studying opera, all of them stared back at me with expressions that were a mixture of misery and terror.

On the second day, however, I could see the boys begin to perk up as soon as I mentioned that certain opera plots involved people being buried alive or knifed to death.

"In fact," I told them, "an opera called *Salome* was considered so vile and disgusting that for a while it was actually banned at the Met."

"How do you spell *Salome*?" Scott asked, quickly grabbing his notebook and writing.

As I continued to share stories involving love triangles, sui-

cides, and betrayal, Amanda said, "Wow, this is like a soap opera!" Her eyes widened and she smiled.

"You mean there are stories?" Andy said earnestly. "I didn't even know they were singing real words. I just thought they were yelling, 'Aaaaahhh!'"

Within a couple of weeks, Anton and Mike practically ran into the room, saying, "Can you play the song from *Porgy and Bess* before class starts?"

To some of the girls' chagrin, these boys sang: "It ain't necessarily soooo . . ."

"You know, I thought opera would be dopey and lame," Jeff said. "But it was pretty cool."

"I told my parents I wanted them to take me to an opera!" Lauren told me.

But what really threw me was when I saw Chris a few months after the class was over.

"Hey, Ms. Blaske," he said. "I bought a book called *Opera for Dummies*. I liked the CD that came with it, but some of those songs are really strange!"

And with that he continued down the hall, lost in a sea of other kids.

Did I hear him right? Chris—a seventh-grade boy—bought a book and CD about opera?

Now I've heard every-
thing!

High-School
Happenings

Too Old for This Job
TERESA BELL KINDRED

Sometimes things happen in the classroom that make you feel older than the American flag. Once I was talking about changes in transportation and how the coming of the railroad helped bring about the end of the Native American way of life.

A girl raised her hand and asked, "Did you ride on the first train across the States?"

"Yeah, sure," I replied. "I used it to escape after my gunfight at the OK Corral."

If the Shoe Fits

Amy Davidson Grubb

Although I'm a teacher, my students are the ones who continually teach me. I'll never forget the day one of them taught me a lesson in humility.

It was the morning of our senior awards assembly at Spotsylvania High School. Seniors lined the hallways in their caps and gowns, ready to file before their parents, teachers, and fellow students to receive their scholarships and awards. I felt a sense of parental pride as I passed a few students I had taught throughout their high-school careers. Had it only been four years ago that these poised young men and women had been gangly, nervous students in my Latin class?

I ducked into my classroom to get the award I was to present. Straightening my dress, I wished I had time to check my hair before taking the stage. On my way to the auditorium, one of the seniors—a young lady I had taught a few years ago—rushed up

 67

to me. She was very upset. "Mrs. Grubb," she said, "I have a huge favor to ask you."

"What?"

She stuck out a sandal-clad foot. "I forgot to wear dress shoes this morning, and they won't let me go through without them." I knew she was right; the senior sponsors had been adamant about the dress code. All seniors had to wear dress clothes under their gowns, with dark-colored, closed-toe shoes.

"I've got to get in there," she continued. "My parents are here. My dad even took off from work because I'm getting an award."

I knew where she was headed before she asked: "Can I borrow your shoes?"

I hesitated, eyeing her sandals—little strappy things with a leather hoop for the big toe. I couldn't wear them with my pantyhose. And I had to make a presentation. How would it look when the Latin teacher strode to the podium in her stocking-clad feet? Still, I looked at her anxious face and kicked off my shoes.

"Thank you so much!" she gushed. "I knew I could count on you!" She ran back to join the seniors.

As I waited my turn onstage, I tried to keep my feet tucked under the chair. I began to think about the reasons I had decided to go into the teaching profession. Sure, I wanted to pass on my love of the Latin language, but what I truly desired was to make a difference in the lives of my students. I wanted them to see that human beings care about each other and that happiness can be found not by focusing on self but on others. This assembly wasn't about me or the remarks I made. It was about recognizing the achievements of these graduates. So when it was my turn to present the award, I proudly stepped up to the podium, my shoeless feet padding across the stage and my student's words ringing in

 68

my ears. "I knew I could count on you!" Wasn't that what it was all about?

After the ceremony, the girl walked toward me, her mother in tow. "Mom," she said, "this is the teacher I was telling you about. When they wouldn't let me into the assembly, I thought of Mrs.Grubb immediately."

I beamed. I really had made a difference in this girl's life. Not only did she know I would help her, but she thought of me before all of her other teachers.

Then she continued: "I remembered that she had big feet."

The Hormone Challenge
Teresa Bell Kindred

One of the things that makes teaching high school such a challenge is the fact that most teenagers are big bundles of hormones. It seems to me drug companies should take some of the students' hormones and inject them into old people. Then teenagers would be less cocky and old folks would have more get-up-and-go.

I guess you could say teenagers are going through a stage. Of course, I've used this excuse about my oldest son's behavior since he was a baby. First, we blamed it on the colic, then on the terrible twos. He just turned thirteen, and he still shows signs of the colic and the terrible twos; only now it's combined with the dreaded puberty. Maybe puberty is just a continuation of the terrible twos with acne and body hair thrown in.

Teenage boys' hormones make them want to impress teenage girls. So they strut around like roosters and claim their territory like guard dogs. When a stray mutt crosses the line, they fight

 70

like wrestlers on late-night television. Teenage boys around here want to drive big trucks (we live in the country) with stereos that have more bass than treble. And above all else, they never, ever want to look like geeks.

On the other hand, teenage girls' hormones dictate that they don't fight as much as they love to be fought over. They love dates who will spend more than three dollars on a movie rental. They're full of gossip and giggles, and they worry constantly about their looks. They like to drive flashy cars and wear clothes that are too tight, too short, or too low. They spend an hour on their hair and ten minutes studying for their history test. And above all else, they never, ever want to look like geeks.

To survive in a classroom full of hormones, the teacher must do certain things. She must stretch her memory back to the days when she was a teenager—and try to outmaneuver them. In other words, figure out what they're going to do and, before they do it, stop it. For instance, never turn off the lights when showing a film, or there might be more action in the back of the room than on the screen.

The teacher doesn't worry about being a geek. All teachers are geeks. That's the nice part about being an adult. You know what the kids think of you, but you don't care.

Homework Hassles

Elaine K. McEwan

My kids had some amazing teachers in their schooling careers. These folks must have stayed awake nights conceiving assignments that would have challenged a college student. Ours was an upwardly mobile school district where all the parents thought their child was gifted, so the teachers rose to the occasion.

Emily and I had barely managed to survive one round of assignments in Mr. Baker's interdisciplinary core class, and I breathed a sigh of relief as she took the project, worthy of a doctoral dissertation, off to school. Perhaps we could enjoy a weekend of family fun and recreation without pressure and deadlines.

I laughingly said to her as she arrived home from school that night, "So, what's the next big assignment in core class, writing the great American novel?"

She looked at me in amazement. "Yeah," she answered. "How did you know?"

Stick to the Subject

Hands Off
JIM VOLLER

My friend Sarah Wilson was teaching her class of fourteen-year-olds the story of King Midas.

Legend tells us that everything King Midas touched turned to gold. It made him very rich, but there was a problem. You see, when Midas's lovely daughter came into the room, he reached out and embraced her. She turned to gold, and Midas was devastated.

After a pause, she asked, "What does that teach us?"

A boy's hand shot up. "Well, I guess it teaches us boys to keep our hands off the girls."

Embellied

Dalene Vickery Parker

Bridgett tore into the classroom and excitedly waved her essay in front of my podium. "Mrs. Parker, Mrs. Parker, I did it. I did what you told me to. I embellied my paper."

I looked up in confusion. "You did what?"

"I did what you told me to. I *embellied* it! I think you'll like it a lot better now. I can't wait for you to read it." Bridgett's words tumbled out in a torrent.

"Bridgett, would you slow down just a minute and explain to me what you mean?" I asked. "It sounds like you ate your paper."

"No, Mrs. Parker, don't you remember? You told me to embelly it—to add more words, fancy it up a little, explain it better. I liked that *embelly* word so much that I told all my other teachers you taught it to me."

"Oh, I see. Well, thank you, dear. I look forward to seeing the changes you made." Outwardly, I smiled as I took Bridgett's

paper. Inwardly, however, I cringed. What other great tidbits of wisdom had students like Bridgett attributed to me as their teacher?

Later, as I wrote responses to Bridgett's embellishments, I realized it didn't matter. She may not have gotten the word right, but she did get the point. Her "embellied" paper was much improved. More important, however, was the way Bridgett had exhibited a rare and wonderful enthusiasm for learning new ideas and sharing them with others. That was something to be proud of, whether I got the proper credit or not.

> What other great tidbits of wisdom had students like Bridgett attributed to me as their teacher?

I don't remember all my students' names, and certainly not their essays, one or two decades later. But Bridgett and her embellied paper will forever stay etched in my mind and heart—or should that be in my stomach?

You Call That History?

Teresa Bell Kindred

I teach history to tenth and eleventh graders. Maybe I should say I try to teach history. Next to being a brain surgeon, I can't imagine a more challenging job. To teenagers history is something that happened last weekend, not fifty or one hundred years ago.

Sometimes the best thing about teaching is that your students are someone else's kids, and at the end of the day, you get to send them home. The worst thing is, after being around teenagers all day who know absolutely everything, you have to go home to your own children, who also know absolutely everything. Sometimes I wonder how I got so stupid. It must have happened right after I realized my own parents weren't as dumb as I thought they were.

Occasionally someone will wake up in the classroom long enough to make an intelligent comment that gives me some encouragement. One day I asked if anyone knew who Joseph

McCarthy was. A tall boy in the back of the room raised his hand and shouted, "I know, Mrs. Kindred, I know. He was one of the Beatles!"

I once spent weeks discussing World War I and felt the students had a pretty good grip on the subject. After we watched a film on the sinking of the *Lusitania*, I gave a test. Imagine my surprise when I read one student's test paper and learned that one event that helped pull America into the war was the sinking of the *Mayflower*. Oh well. At least he knew the *Lusitania* was a ship that sank.

Nathan was sitting at my desk—which was a no-no— but he was behaving, so I let it slide

Another time we spent two weeks studying the westward movement during the 1800s. When it came time for the test, I asked students to write an essay using certain key words, including *Dust Bowl*. One of my less-attentive students explained that the Dust Bowl was a college football game. Sometimes I wonder just what it would take to get through to some of them.

There's always one student who comes just a little closer to driving you crazy than the others. For me, this was Nathan. It wasn't that Nathan disliked me or that he disliked history. He was just too busy being an entertainer to pay much attention to the lesson. One day I was standing before the class, reviewing for a test. Nathan was sitting at my desk—which was a no-no—but he was behaving, so I let it slide. Or at least I thought he was behaving.

"Mrs. Kindred, look," he yelled gleefully.

I looked, and so did the class. A few days earlier, I had worn pierced earrings that were too heavy. They were the long, dangly kind, and I felt like the weight of them had stretched my ear lobes until they were longer than my hair. I took them off and put them in my desk drawer. Nathan had found one and put it through a piercing in his left nostril. As I stared in dull horror, he shook it at me.

I could never make myself wear those earrings again.

Discerning Minds Want to Know

Elizabeth Delayne

Like most teachers, I'll do whatever it takes to make my lesson more than just mumbling words students think they hear. I use Microsoft PowerPoint presentations packed with photographs and maps. I have the students complete group projects, illustrations, and take-home projects. We use the Internet, and we go to the library. We sing about the War of 1812, we dance the Charleston, and sometimes—OK, most of the time—we take notes.

The World Wide Web has taken the study of history to an exciting new level. It's easy to find maps, photographs, and information to project on the wall and put on work sheets. Lesson plans are easily shared. Teachers and students have access to professional journals and other material compiled by people as far away as another continent. Students have a treasure house of knowledge at their fingertips for study and research.

With so much information, sometimes you have to limit the Web sites a student can visit. The quantity of facts can easily overwhelm even the most discerning minds. But sometimes you wish students had opened a few more links—or possibly their textbooks.

I assigned each student to create an illustrated dictionary of terms, names, and issues on the subject of imperialism. Students could use the Internet to copy and paste pictures, diagrams, or other illustrations along with their research. The day came for the students to turn in their work. I took up notebook after notebook until I came to one student who sat on the front row—not by choice, mind you.

"Ms. Delayne," he said as he handed me his assignment, "I found out where you get all your information!"

I paused and looked at him. "Where?" I asked.

"From *Encarta!*"

Encarta—the electronic encyclopedia. The secret was out. I, a history teacher with a college degree, get my information from an encyclopedia. Well, at least he finally knows I'm not making it up.

Spelling Lesson
Kathryn Lay

It was my first experience homeschooling a child . . . my child.
I could tell she was ready to start learning. She loved listening
to stories and making up her own, even though she couldn't
read. She enjoyed simple math as I put one and one of her
favorite stuffed animals or dolls together to make two.

She was even more thrilled as she began recognizing and
spelling simple words. Her favorite was S-T-O-P. Every trip to
the store or library or mall included her spelling this exciting
word as she pointed to the big red sign. Soon she was spelling
B-E-D and D-O-G and C-A-T.

I was thrilled, too, about teaching my daughter and watching
her excitement.

Then one day as we sat coloring together, she asked, "Mom,
what does D-Z-P-L-M spell?"

I smiled and said, "Nothing."

Soon after, as we drove into a parking lot, she shouted from her car seat, "Mom, what does E-B-T-R spell?"

"Nothing," I explained. I worried that she would get frustrated with her attempts at spelling out of the blue.

This went on for several days, but she never faltered, never frowned when I said, "Nothing."

Then one afternoon we were waiting in line at the bank drive-through. I wasn't surprised when Michelle popped up with, "Mama, what does B-D-R-Z spell?"

I sighed and shook my head. "I'm sorry, sweetheart, that spells nothing."

She grinned and proclaimed, "There sure are a lot of ways to spell *nothing*."

I knew I still had a lot to learn about teaching.

Those Amazing Subs

Any Volunteers?
Margaret N. Windley

Both teachers for our Sunday school class announced they would be away for a few weeks. At the end of the class, a call went out for a volunteer to teach the next Sunday. No one stirred; everyone looked at the floor, their feet, or the furniture. I had to chuckle when I turned to the following week's lesson and saw the title: "Overcoming Reluctance to Lead."

How Hard Can This Be?

Margolyn Woods

The phone startled me.

"Could you possibly substitute for my class today?" asked my son's kindergarten teacher. "I have a family emergency, and I can't locate any of our regular subs."

As a stay-at-home mom, I was flattered. *How hard can this be?* I thought. After all, it was only for one day.

"Sure," I responded. I'd never been a teacher, but I had worked for fifteen years before having children. And I did have three children of my own.

As I walked into the classroom, the bell rang. Before I could sit down, two sweet-looking little girls approached. "Can we go to the bathroom?" they asked.

"Sure," I said, unaware of the one-at-a-time rule.

The morning started off relatively smoothly. Then a neighboring teacher popped her head in the door and announced that

the toilets were all stopped up. I learned about the one-at-a-time rule and set off to find maintenance while she watched over both of our classrooms.

Lunchtime was a new experience. It was pizza day, and most of the kids at my table simply had a slice of pizza and two or three cartons of chocolate milk. Several, however, opted for pudding and chocolate milk for lunch. Most of the children wore pizza back to the classroom.

The afternoon dragged on as one child cried that it was her turn to be the door monitor and another swore it was his. I was beginning to realize the incredible talent it took to keep seventeen children interested and excited about learning. My son loved this class, and he loved Mrs. Winnie. She had not only gained the respect of seventeen five-year-olds, but she had stretched them to follow inquisitive thoughts, and she had sparked new interests.

I have to admit I began watching the clock as we got closer to the end of the day. Not just so I could go home, but so I could sit down. I was exhausted. As the last child went out the door, I grabbed my coat and purse. Just then, one small girl ran back inside. She threw her arms around me and gave me a big hug.

"I love you," she said as she let go and once again headed for the door.

My heart soared. I wouldn't have missed this for the world.

As soon as I got home, I propped up my feet and wrote notes of appreciation to each of my children's teachers.

Classroom Riot

Amber Ferguson

My daughter had the same wonderful teacher in both second and third grade. Whenever she needed a substitute, the teacher asked one of the mothers to fill in. After the first year passed and I received no invitation to substitute, my feelings were a little hurt.

Now I know why she waited so long before calling me. I think teachers who survive the job for twenty years or more must develop a sixth sense when it comes to judging character.

My chance to sub came the second year, when this lovely lady wanted to leave early for Thanksgiving break. Whether all the other mothers were busy, sick, or in jail at the time, I'll never know. But she was desperate enough to allow me to bring along my preschooler.

The schedule was simple, and my job started out well enough. Playground time was the first order of business, but a chilly breeze was blowing and the children complained almost at once.

 89

My instructions were that the children could watch a movie if the weather was poor, so I led them back inside.

Fifteen minutes into my tenure, and so far so good.

I checked the movie inventory and asked the little darlings which one they wanted to watch. No kid wanted to see the same movie as any other kid. After a heated debate, during which the rule against name-calling was broken, I gave up and moved on to the next item on the schedule: reading to the children.

With thirty minutes under my belt and a crisis averted, I was still doing OK. Although I wondered what I would do when I'd gone through the lesson plan. I was already two hours ahead of schedule.

Remembering the movie controversy, I appraised the stash of books without asking for opinions. Frankly, they looked boring. I had a picky crowd on my hands, so I skimmed the room for something else to read. One of the boys, halo gleaming, offered me his library book: a large, glossy picture book about snakes.

Hoping that might keep them interested for two hours, I instructed the children to sit in a semicircle around my chair. As I read snake facts aloud in a bright, happy voice, I often turned the book around to show pictures to the class.

The little dears were appropriately enthralled.

A photo of a water moccasin reminded me of the time I'd surprised one in my flowerbed, so I related the incident to the kids. Even as they squealed over my horror story, they all raised their hands in the air, calling my name, begging to tell a snake anecdote of their own.

I conceded, thinking I would allow them to speak in an orderly fashion. Within seconds I was the only person still sitting. Most of the children were standing on tiptoe, hands in the

air; a few were jumping up and down, and one boy was jumping on a chair. I was also the only one who remembered what an "inside voice" was, but I quickly had to abandon mine to be heard over competing shouts.

"Mrs. Ferguson! Let me tell about my rattlesnake rattle—"

"Mrs. Ferguson! Mrs. Ferguson! My dad once got bit by a copperhead—"

My preschooler, no fan of noisy mobs, even when they're not rioting, began screaming hysterically just about the time the principal stormed in.

Now for the worst part. I didn't tell you everything. First, most classes have twenty or more students. But this school was tiny. There were only eight children in the class—and one of them was my own. If that's not bad enough, I wasn't even substituting all day. My job was from noon until 3:00 p.m. Only three hours.

So I admit it. I completely lost control of eight previously well-behaved children in roughly one hour. After I stopped shaking, I realized my admiration for teachers had increased significantly.

But I'd rather clean every toilet in Texas than spend one second in a classroom again myself.

Not that I've been asked.

Which Witch?

Marti Kramer Suddarth

One of the joys (and hazards) of working with young children is that they always let me know exactly where I stand. An adult may feign friendliness while secretly planning my demise, but preschoolers practice no such deceit. Though they rarely hold grudges, these tots tend to say what they think and mean what they say. Working with young children isn't for the thin-skinned. I learned this lesson the old-fashioned way while subbing as a teacher's assistant for a class of four-year-olds. It was the middle of October, and the children were chattering away about their Halloween costume plans as they colored and stickered their work sheets.

"I'm going to be a cowboy," one young man announced.

"My mom is making me a bride's dress," said an angelic-faced little girl.

Others made their selections from Saturday morning cartoons and department-store shelves. Superman and Cinderella were classic choices, but it was the 1980s and many of their ideas reflected the times. Several boys hoped to dress as Lion-O or He-Man, while a number of girls chose Cheetara and She-Ra.

I listened for a while, and then emboldened by their enthusiasm, I decided to join in. Thinking they'd find it humorous to imagine a grownup in costume, I asked, "What do you think I should be?"

One little girl spoke right up. "A witch."

Though they rarely hold grudges, these tots tend to say what they think and mean what they say.

A witch? A cackling, toil-and-trouble-brewing, children-for-breakfast-eating witch? Did they really think I was that mean? Ready to take my lumps, I laughed nervously and asked, "Why do you think I should be a witch?"

Then in that naive, brutally honest way most four-year-olds have of speaking their minds, my would-be costume designer looked up from her coloring and innocently replied, "Because you have a long, pointy nose."

At least I knew where I stood.

Second-Grade Theology
Elaine Mitchell

I was once asked to teach religion to a classroom full of second graders for a twelve-week period because their teacher was on maternity leave. I readily accepted and excitedly and prayerfully prepared my lessons. For the first few days, the children were kind of quiet as they sized me up. I enthusiastically showed them my love for God, and they began to relax.

During the second week, they started asking questions. I was thrilled with their curiosity and tried to answer respectfully and to the best of my ability. I did fine until little Joey started asking the questions.

"Who is God?"

"He's our creator," I responded. "He made us. He is full of goodness and love."

Another hand went up. "Where does he live?"

"Well, some say he lives in heaven, but God is not limited—he lives inside each of us. He's everywhere."

"How can he be everywhere at once?"

"Because he's God, and he can do all things."

"But how do we know there is a God?"

"We believe in God—we use our gift of faith. Jesus came to earth to teach us about his Father and the love he has for each of us."

"Is he a person?"

"Is he a spirit?"

"What is he?"

"Does he eat?"

"Does he sleep?"

The questions came as fast as I could answer them. Hands were raised all over the room, and I tried to give everyone a chance to speak. Joey's hand went up again.

I did fine
until little Joey
started asking
the question.

"Why can't we see him?" he demanded.

"Why can't we see him?" I repeated the question out loud to give myself time to think.

More hands were going up all over the room. I needed help. I called on the Holy Spirit for guidance—the last thing I wanted to do was to be untrue to these children or to God.

I saw a persistent hand waving. "What is it, Hannah?"

"I know why we can't see God," she said.

"OK, Hannah, why can't we see God?"

"We can't see God because we were born with veils over our eyes. As we get older and learn more about God, our veil will

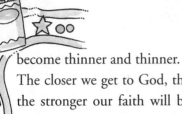

become thinner and thinner. We'll learn to love God and others. The closer we get to God, the thinner our veil will become and the stronger our faith will be. But we'll never see God clearly until our veil is completely removed. On that day we will be in heaven with Jesus."

My eyes were glazed over as I thanked Hannah (and the Holy Spirit) for this intervention. I told Hannah I believed she was absolutely right and asked her where she had learned that.

"My mom told me," she replied matter-of-factly.

Of Parents
and Principals

Be Nice

DORIS JOHNSON

I once shared my job as school secretary with a terrific lady named Julie. When she quit, I took over full time in the office. One little guy—a first grader—stopped by the office nearly every day at noon for a week. He would come in, peer over the counter, look puzzled, then walk out again.

Finally one day I asked the boy if he needed some help.

"Where's the nice secretary?" he asked.

The Apple Doesn't Fall Far

Brenda Nixon

As a speaker, writer, and teacher on parenting, I often have the opportunity to witness the truth in the adage "The apple doesn't fall far from the tree." One of those opportunities occurred on a crisp, autumn night in a crowded school auditorium. I was scheduled to speak to an audience of elementary kids' parents on the topic of discipline. Prior to the start of the evening's event, the program planner and I were talking privately.

"We have a large group here tonight," she observed with a sparkle in her eye.

"It's gratifying to see so many parents wanting to learn about effective discipline," I replied.

"I hope we get through all of your good information," she whispered. "Sometimes they start asking too many questions and get the speaker off track."

"Let's ensure that the information gets out and everyone has time to hear it by asking them to hold questions until the end of the program," I suggested.

"OK, that's a plan," she agreed.

Soon she stood at the podium to introduce me. Politely she announced, "We have so much material to cover tonight, I want to make sure Brenda has a chance to share it, so please hold all your questions until the end of her presentation."

After some awkward moments of my talking and his relentless motioning, his wife pulled down his hand.

She stepped aside and signaled for me to take the floor. I stood at the podium and opened my mouth to begin. Instantly, one father waved his hand to indicate a question. I shared my first point, ignoring his gesture. After some awkward moments of my talking and his relentless motioning, his wife pulled down his hand.

I finished my talk on children and discipline, then asked, "Does anyone have questions?"

Immediately, the same man motioned to me again. Looking at him in acknowledgment I said, "Yes, how can I help?"

He responded, "My son never listens to the rules!"

Tuna Yule
Karen Cogan

Wanting to personalize my daughter Tiffany's holiday gift for her Sunday school teacher, I decided to make homemade Christmas cookies. I baked the cookies a few days in advance, storing them in a recycled margarine tub in the refrigerator.

The Sunday before Christmas I hurriedly grabbed the container, wrapped it, and added a red bow.

When we returned home from church, my husband, John, began digging in the refrigerator for lunch possibilities.

"There's some leftover tuna in a container," I said.

A minute later, he emerged with a puzzled look. "The only container I can find is full of Christmas cookies."

My daughter's teacher ended up with festively wrapped tuna.

In the Office with Jason

Elaine K. McEwan

Jason, an intense first grader, was sitting at the round table in my office with his parents. Jason was already a social outcast at the tender age of six, and I could tell that his parents were defensive. Surely if I were a better principal and his teacher were more effective, Jason would have loads of friends and be having a great year in first grade.

Jason had received a detention from the art teacher for hitting one of his classmates. His parents were protesting the unfairness of Jason's consequence. He assured his parents that he had done no such thing. They were mystified as to why we were picking on Jason. Obviously we had a serious communication breakdown here. I needed the wisdom of Solomon and the eloquence of Churchill to come out of this conference alive. Suddenly I had an inspiration. I would ask Jason to reenact the scene for me. Perhaps the truth would come out. Jason was eager to participate.

"I didn't do anything," he assured me. "She wouldn't leave me alone."

"What did she do?" I asked.

His parents were silent observers.

"Well," Jason said slowly, "she put her elbow in my space."

"Like this?" I demonstrated, sliding my elbow into his "space."

"Yeah," he agreed with a big smile.

"So, what did you do then?" I asked.

"Oh, nothing," he said.

"Show me," I suggested.

Jason cocked his elbow and slammed it into the side of my body. He was not subtle.

Both of his parents were wide-eyed.

"Well," I said, "I think that solves the problem of what happened. Would you both agree that Jason will be staying after school?"

Smoking in the Boys' Room

Laurie Copeland

How do teachers strike that delicate balance between maintaining classroom control, having fun with their students, and not pulling out their chalk-dusted hair in the process? Bill Barker instinctively knew how to accomplish that difficult task. As a teacher and principal at the elementary, high-school, and college levels, he combined his sense of humor with his disciplinary obligations.

After he retired, Bill was asked to be an interim principal at Greece Olympia High School, where he had taught many years earlier. The administrators knew of his love for the students and his silly shenanigans that made school a fun place to attend, and they were having serious discipline problems. Bill was the man for the job.

One day Bill was walking down the hallway toward his office when a pungent smell drifted out of the boys' bathroom: ciga-

rette smoke. He immediately detoured into the tiled room.

A lone young man was there, quickly stuffing something into his jeans pocket. He looked so guilty that Bill's scheming sense of humor took over. He engaged him in a lengthy conversation as smoke curled up and out of the student's pocket. The boy became increasingly uneasy, rocking from one foot to the other. Finally, face twisted, he let out a yelp and yanked his hand from his pocket, dragging with it the smoldering remains of a Lucky Strike.

He engaged him in a lengthy conversation as smoke curled up and out of the student's pocket.

It was weeks before the student could see any humor in his trip to the bathroom. But ultimately he did—and thought twice before ever lighting up again!

Sometimes being a good teacher means simply knowing how to outwit 'em.

There Are Bad Days …
and Then There's Teaching

Pet Peeves
ANITA CORRINE DONIHUE

Mrs. Foster, a teacher at my school, had a frustrating day with one of her first-grade boys. "You've been doing irritating things all day today. These things are some of my pet peeves," she said sternly. "Do you know what a pet peeve is?"

The little boy shook his head no.

"A pet peeve is the thing that irritates a person the most. Do you know what my pet peeve is?" she asked.

The boy paused. "Ummm...Mr. Foster?"

The Bug in the Basement
Carol Chaffee Fielding

My classroom was in the basement. "It makes sense," the headmaster had said, "to put the photo classroom and darkroom in the darkest part of the building."

Wonderful. The one and only basement classroom would become my classroom and lab. I liked the sound of it until I went down there for the first time. When I flipped the light switch, little bugs scurried under the desk and table and . . . everywhere! The smell reminded me of when I've done laundry in the summertime and then forgotten the load in the washing machine for a few days. The classroom would need a lot of work, but since I'd finally have one of my own, I wouldn't complain. With just one week to go till summer vacation, I decided I'd clean and paint it just before school started back up in the fall.

But when I returned to paint it, I found that the school's maintenance workers had taken it upon themselves to paint the

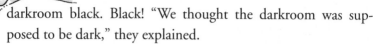

darkroom black. Black! "We thought the darkroom was supposed to be dark," they explained.

I looked around—the floors, walls, ceilings, and tables—everything was black. Looking around, I realized that I couldn't see the bugs, even with the lights on. They blended in with their surroundings.

Classes went smoothly for the first few months. The students settled into a routine and were producing good quality prints. Occasionally, various students would report that some bug had wandered into a tray of chemicals and embalmed itself and ask me to please clean it out.

Masses of cobwebs filled the corners. Silverfish occasionally wandered onto the ceiling, and a stray peppermint candy once brought a neat line of ants. All of this provided photo subjects for my students. Then winter came and, with it, a bug I will never forget.

Then winter came and, with it, a bug I will never forget.

"Mrs. Fiiiiieeeeelding!" Sammie bolted through the light trap and crossed the twenty-foot room in about three bounds. Grabbing my arm, she shrieked, "There's a bug back there—a huge bug! I've never seen anything so big!" Her eyes were like saucers, and she was shaking. By now, others were exiting the darkroom. No one else had seen the bug, and everyone talked at once:

"Where did you see it?"

"What did it look like?"

"How big was it?"

Sammie composed herself enough to answer their questions. "On the easel of the enlarger. It was big and long and had lots of legs." She paused and shuddered. "It crawled right in front of me when I was trying to adjust the light. It almost ran over my hand!"

A search party was organized, and the selected students returned to the darkroom, flashlights in hand. Sammie stayed in the classroom, flatly refusing to set foot in the darkroom until the creature had been captured or squished. The remaining twenty minutes of class was lost as the fearless hunters sought this mammoth of the twenty-first century. When the bell rang, they all gave a collective "Aaaawwww!" The hunt ended.

The next day, after a bit of coaxing, Sammie returned to the darkroom. The bug stayed out of sight for a while—long enough for most people to forget or to chalk up the sighting to an overactive imagination. The students teased Sammie, who responded with an angry, "I know what I saw. It's still here; I just know it. You'll see!"

Nearly three weeks later, I was lecturing with my back to the classroom, writing on the marker board. Behind me, I heard someone gasp. "Look, look, look!"

I turned to see Diane pointing to the floor at the front of the room—near me. Sammie looked up from her notes and was up on the table within half a second. "I told you! I told you it was real!" she said as she reached down to retrieve her backpack from the floor.

When I finally looked, my blood froze. I was actually afraid to move. I've never been bug-phobic, but this thing really freaked me out. It reminded me of something I had seen in a 1960s sci-fi television rerun.

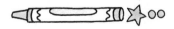

The creature was at least two inches long with lots of little legs on both sides of its body, which had two white stripes running the length of it. It was walking—no, sprinting—across the tile floor at an amazing speed, antennas straight out in front. One student, Lee, stepped forward and unceremoniously slammed his hiking boot down on the bug. When he lifted his foot, we all spoke in unison. "Eww!"

A sizable brown stain remained on the floor, along with a few disembodied legs.

"OK, Sam, we believe you now," Lee said.

"Thanks for getting rid of it, Lee."

"That thing was raunchy!"

"Gruesome."

And then someone had to say, "I hope there aren't any more."

Diane jumped up from her stool. "Mrs. Fielding, may I go to the library? I want to find out what that thing was." As soon as the bell rang, they were off like thoroughbreds at Belmont, racing to the library and logging onto the Internet.

The next day Diane entered the classroom and said, "*Scutigera coleoptrata.*"

"What?"

"That's what it's called in Latin. *Scutigera coleoptrata.* It's a house centipede, and it likes to live in dark places. The Web site I found says that no amount of pesticide will get rid of them."

"Wow. So they're like roaches?"

"Nope," Diane smiled, glad to be the one providing the information rather than taking notes. "Unlike roaches, they don't live on garbage—they're carnivores; they eat other bugs."

It's been three years since I first encountered this fearsome creature, and it still curdles my blood whenever I see one ventur-

ing out into the open. (Oh yes, there were more.) I learned that for every *Scutigera coleoptrata* I see, there are approximately twenty that I don't see. Of course, I never shared that information with my classes—or they'd never enter the darkroom again!

News spread around campus of the strange inhabitants of the darkroom (besides the students, that is). Diane was right—no amount of bug spray kept these things away. I used a whole can around the perimeter of the room. Sticky traps don't work either because the bug will just leave a few legs behind, which just makes you feel guilty for putting out traps resulting in a centipede with a limp.

Some of the students have captured one of these bugs and named it Fred; others have been content to take photos of them—when they actually stop running across the floor. I've received numerous prints of the little monsters, all of which made me nauseated, but I graded them nonetheless. The environmental science teacher and I even combined our classes once. My students showed off their prints—and Fred himself—while his class gave reports on centipedes.

While there surely is a reason for the existence of every living thing, no matter how small, large, or creepy, some of them are best left to the darker corners. I'm sure God is getting a kick out of every time one of the little beasts scurries across my classroom floor, raising the hair on the back of my neck.

Maybe that's the reason for its existence—to make God chuckle as I madly run away from a two-inch bug.

Trailer Living
Teresa Bell Kindred

The first few years of my teaching career, I was a floating teacher. No, that doesn't mean I taught underwater basket weaving. There weren't enough classrooms at our school, so I was assigned to other teachers' classrooms during their planning periods. This situation is far from ideal. Not only do you have to carry a ton of books and papers with you, but you can never remember just where you're supposed to be. Several times I would begin a class only to have some wise guy in the front seat say, "Yo, Teacher. This is algebra class, not history."

After two years I was given my own classroom. It was a run-down trailer with holes in the floor and rotten doors. Still, I got to stay in one location. There were two doors to the trailer, one on each end. To keep kids from escaping when I turned my back, I placed my desk in the middle of the trailer and paced back and forth, side to side. I only lost a few students this way, and they

were ones I wanted to lose. You know, the real troublemakers. The ones other students rat on because they can't stand them either. Alas, after they realized I wasn't coming to look for them, they got bored with hide-and-seek and came back to class.

The trailer had its own personality. In the winter we had to combat the cold. The wall heaters would burn those sitting next to them while the rest of us froze. More than once I had to stop class to put out a fire where someone sat too close to the heater. The only time this posed a problem was when Chrissy's pants caught on fire. They were so tight she couldn't drop and roll. All the boys in the class volunteered to smother the fire.

I once had my world history class write a paper entitled "What I Would Put in My Tomb." We had just finished talking about the pharaohs of Egypt and what they had placed in their tombs. All Chrissy wanted in her tomb was a can of hair spray and her makeup.

Another time, the wall heater fell out of the wall during class. It sounded like a bomb going off. It was the same wall the air conditioner was in, so I expected it to fall out too, but it never did. The kids had cemented it to the wall with their bubblegum.

If the wind blew very hard, we shook. It reminded me of the trailer Bill and I lived in right after we got married. When the washer went through the spin cycle, you had to hold on to something or you'd fall off the couch.

Only once did our class have to leave the trailer and go into the main building because of wind. The sky was pitch-black, and the trailer was shaking like a leaf. Even in the building, the students were huddled in the halls with their heads between their legs. All I could think of was my own children, who were at the grade school down the road. Were they scared? Were they crying

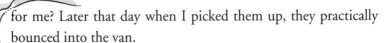
for me? Later that day when I picked them up, they practically bounced into the van.

"Hi, Mom. Great day, wasn't it? We got to sit in the hall and cover our heads. It was a blast!"

Warmer weather brought visitors to my classroom trailer. In addition to insects from the rotting wood, the holes in the floor were home to a family of mice, and sometimes they would come out and entertain us. I found out much later that the students were bringing part of their lunches back to the trailer and stuffing it down the holes in the floor to feed the rodents.

One day during my lecture, I realized my students were actually awake. They were showing signs of interest, so I really got into what I was saying. I waved my arms, pointed to maps, and discussed technology in warfare. At last I realized the students weren't focused on me; it was something behind me. I turned and looked. Three mice were playing tag just a few feet away. I told the students whoever could get rid of the mice got an A for the day, and then I left the trailer.

I never saw any mice after that.

Standing Ovation
Bianca Elliott

I have a reputation at school for being unflappable. I'm not sure how this reputation began, but I reap the benefits of it shamelessly.

One day I was going to instruct my above-average students in some fine point of Spanish. This would necessitate me calling upon the ELMO machine. Now you must understand certain points about ELMOs. We Americans live in the most powerful society in the world. We educate each and every child, no matter what his or her particular needs or abilities are. We achieve stunning success with materials that really haven't changed much in about two hundred years: a blackboard, chalk, textbooks, and . . . an overhead machine. ELMOs are overhead projectors. It's my contention that there are teachers who can't teach unless they have ELMO in their classroom.

Since I don't often use ELMOs in class, I usually get the ones that are almost ready to be retired—like some of the faculty. Well, for this upcoming instructional experience, I needed ELMO's specific skills.

I was instructing the students and walking toward my ELMO. I continued the lesson while I prepared him for service as I had done many times. As I placed my hand on ELMO's cart to move him, I noticed that one of his legs wasn't facing the right direction. No matter, it would still work. I started to pull ELMO to his proper location when the wheel fell out. I don't know how; it just did.

The machine was open in places I didn't think were appropriate for high-school students to see.

As if in slow motion, I watched ELMO's demise. First the leg came off. Then the machine slid from the stand, and gravity took over. When ELMO hit the floor, parts fell everywhere. The glass from the screen somehow fell out without breaking. The machine was open in places I didn't think were appropriate for high-school students to see.

It wasn't pretty.

What happened next, though, was pretty cool.

The students were watching me, hoping I would cuss like the other teachers or maybe cry or something. Nothing happened. I just looked at poor ELMO's innards. Almost in unison, the students started clapping. Then they rose and gave ELMO a standing ovation for his years of dedicated service. As ELMO was removed from the room, I thought I heard "Taps" being hummed.

I tried to return to the lesson. The students, however, wanted to talk about what had just happened.

"You didn't get upset. You didn't get mad or cuss or nothing."

"Anything," I corrected.

"Yeah, but you know. Why didn't you?"

I wasn't sure what to say. What would you say?

"Things don't matter; people do." They didn't look convinced.

"Look, all that really matters in life is people. Things come and go; records and awards get broken; everything seems to fall apart. But people last, and I believe they'll last forever. So things aren't that important as long as the people are safe. Does that make sense?" I looked at the class.

Some students just had dreamy smiles on their faces. Others looked sad. A couple of them weren't sure what was going on. (There are at least two in every class.)

I didn't realize how deeply this incident had affected the students until later in the year. Periodically, I would overhear comments about how I don't get upset about things—that I just care about people. I think ELMO helped my reputation.

Thanks ELMO, and rest in peace.

The Sharpening Demon
Brandy S. Brow

I made the decision during a long, tendonitis-filled episode of sharpening dozens of colored pencils by hand. As a homeschooling mother, I was on a quest: provide my kids something to fill the small, white spaces of their coloring assignments, without grossly running over the lines.

After months of deliberation, I felt that the pain in my hand justified the expense. That is, I had to buy an electric sharpener—if I could move my fingers enough to sign the credit-card slip.

Shortly after I brought the blue monster home, I became enthralled with how quickly it produced a point. The hours of using my finger-held sharpener were finally over. Life couldn't be sweeter.

Later I inserted a pencil and heard an unusual sound. I pulled it out. It was unsharpened and had an emerald green ring around the point. Upon removing the dispenser, I found green crayon

melted into the blades. I spent an hour with a pair of tweezers trying to scrape out the firmly applied wax and wondering, *Who put what into this pencil sharpener?* Nothing could have prepared me, though, for what followed.

Krrrrrrrr. Scratch, scratch, scratch. Eee, eee, eee, eee, eee. Krrrrrrrrr. Scratch, scratch, scratch. Krrr—

"Enough, already!" I hollered.

My purchase had apparently produced a kid addicted to sharpening. How could I have known or suspected? (I had gone to public school, and we weren't allowed to get up and sharpen our pencils every minute.) State guidelines required no training in recognizing the symptoms of pencil-sharpening addiction.

Sure, we homeschooling parents don't have to worry about our kids handling peer pressure at school, but some of us have other wickedness to worry about—keeping pencils and crayons from being mercilessly sacrificed to the Sharpening Demon.

I thought I was smart and efficient when I bought our electric sharpener. Now I'm wondering which will cost more in the long run—pencils or wrist surgery?

The Bomb Exercise

Len Woods

One wintry Sunday morning in the early 1980s, I was leading a youth Sunday school class in a discussion about priorities. I wanted them to think about their lives in light of Christ's commandment to love God with all your heart and to love others as you love yourself (Matthew 22:37–40). My hope was that they might walk away with a renewed commitment to deep relationships—both with God and with people.

To stimulate interest I had the group do an exercise I called, for lack of a better title, The Bomb. The scenario I gave went something like this: "The Kremlin has decided that this particular group of teens is too threatening—too good looking, with too much talent and too much leadership ability. You guys have the potential to change the world, and the Russians know it. So they've launched a preemptive small-scale nuclear strike—just on this one classroom. In fifteen minutes we'll be obliterated.

However, the good news is that we have this special atomic-proof paper that can withstand such a blast. We're going to use the next fourteen-and-a-half minutes to write short notes to the people in our lives who mean the most to us. We don't have time to discuss trivial matters like the weather. This is your chance to say what's on your heart. Begin writing now. Don't dillydally!"

With that bit of instruction, the students began writing feverishly. The room was deathly quiet. The Bomb exercise was a huge hit (no pun intended). Following the "blast," right there at ground zero, we had a great discussion about priorities, about why we fritter our lives away on superficial stuff. We ended the exercise with a challenge to live every day like it might be our last, to focus on people and not things.

A few months passed. It was a Monday in summer, my day off, and I was playing golf (badly, as I recall). When I arrived home, there were several urgent phone messages for me to call Jennifer's mom. My roommate added that everyone—the pastor, parents of several teens, and the associate pastor—had been frantic to find me.

I picked up the phone and dialed Jennifer's number.

No answer.

I called one of my colleagues to find out what was going on.

"Len, we've got a crisis on our hands. Jennifer left last night on a flight to go visit a friend in Texas."

"Right . . ." This had been a planned and parent-approved trip.

"Well, this morning her mother went into her bedroom and found what appears to be a suicide note on her desk."

"What?" I blurted. "Jennifer? No way. I can't see that in a million years. What does the note say?"

"Well, it's pretty grim, along the lines of 'Mom, I'll never see you again. I'll be in heaven soon. But I want you to know a few things. I'm sorry for all the times I've treated you badly. I love you so much. Thank you for everything you've done for me. I wish we could have had many more years together, but there's no way out. Please don't be sad. I'm OK. Take care. I love you. Jennifer.'"

It still didn't register in my mind. "I can't believe that. Jennifer's solid as a rock. I don't see any way she'd do anything like this."

"Yeah, well, when her mom couldn't get in contact with you or anyone at the friend's home in Texas, she hopped a flight to Dallas. She's hoping she can get there in time."

I racked my brain, trying to make sense of all this. Then suddenly the proverbial light bulb clicked on inside my head.

"Wait a minute!" I blurted. "I bet that 'suicide note' was part of a Sunday school exercise we did a few months back."

"You had the kids write suicide notes?"

"No!" I explained the exercise. The more we talked, the more my hunch made sense. Sure enough, within a few hours, a very surprised daughter and a very relieved mother were embracing— 450 miles from home. A giant misunderstanding. A costly mess. But a happy ending.

The moral of the story? Make sure all creative learning exercises are clearly labeled Youth Group Lesson!

Beyond the Call
of Duty

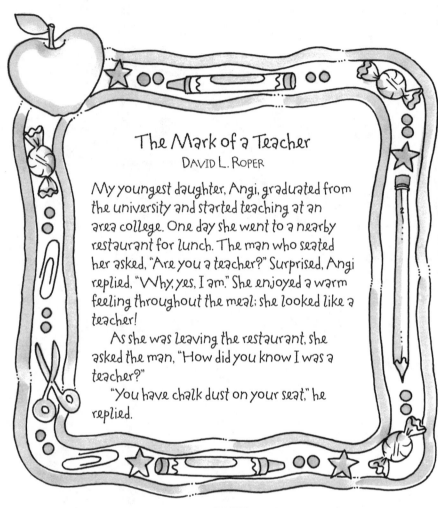

The Mark of a Teacher
DAVID L. ROPER

My youngest daughter, Angi, graduated from the university and started teaching at an area college. One day she went to a nearby restaurant for lunch. The man who seated her asked, "Are you a teacher?" Surprised, Angi replied, "Why, yes, I am." She enjoyed a warm feeling throughout the meal; she looked like a teacher!

As she was leaving the restaurant, she asked the man, "How did you know I was a teacher?"

"You have chalk dust on your seat," he replied.

Frosty Chaperone
Teresa Bell Kindred

I'm not sure how I got the job of Beta Club sponsor. I think I said, "I might consider it." The next thing I knew, I was a sponsor. I enjoyed parts of it. Two other teachers were cosponsors, which made it easier.

The state convention was always held at the same hotel, right before Christmas. Every year we took thirty or forty kids to compete in different events. And every year I came home swearing I wouldn't go back.

One year we were competing in the talent contest, and our skit had a Western theme. Wyatt Earp pulled out his gun in the hotel lobby, and we spent two hours talking to security officers and begging them not to throw us out.

Of course, every year there's the battle over curfew. No teenager I have ever known wants to go to bed before 4:00 a.m. at the state Beta convention. No sponsor I have ever known

 127

wants to stay up that late. Once we had the misfortune of accommodations with an outside balcony that connected all the rooms. Twenty floors in that hotel, and we got the one that gives the kids access to each other's rooms.

There were three sponsors, and we patrolled the halls and rooms better than Kojak or Columbo. Mr. Martin particularly enjoyed his role as an undercover agent. He had been the Beta sponsor long enough that he knew the ropes pretty well. While I

We patrolled the halls and rooms better than Kojak or Columbo.

checked the girls' rooms for contraband or members of the opposite sex, he checked the boys' rooms.

After thirty minutes or so, I was walking by a room when I heard a weak "Help!" I peeked in, and through an outside window I could see the three hairs on top of Mr. Martin's head blowing in the cold December breeze. He had gone to check the balcony and locked himself

out. It was fifteen degrees outside. It took an hour to defrost him, and the other sponsor and I had to finish the room checks. Some people will go to any length to get out of their responsibilities.

Things Aren't What They Seem

Bianca Elliott

Sometimes I don't know how I get in these situations. My husband thinks I have a Pick Her sign over my head. All I know is that on this particular Saturday morning I was scared—a little.

I taught a high-school girls' Sunday school class at church. We elected one Saturday to meet downtown and spend the morning just shopping, or "fellowshipping" (as the Southern Baptists call anything they do in groups of three or more). It was springtime, the girls had money, and the Plaza downtown was beckoning, "Come, spend money . . . come, spend money." Without the business crowd clogging up traffic, I thought it would be fun—forgetting this was a sale weekend at the Plaza. The girls gathered, and we started on our mission to bond. Lots of stores, lots of color. Lots of rich people with too much time on their hands and poor people who wanted to be thought of as rich. (We were in that second set of people.)

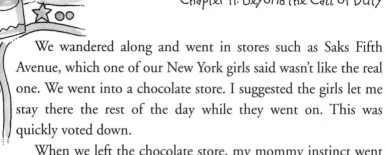

We wandered along and went in stores such as Saks Fifth Avenue, which one of our New York girls said wasn't like the real one. We went into a chocolate store. I suggested the girls let me stay there the rest of the day while they went on. This was quickly voted down.

When we left the chocolate store, my mommy instinct went into overdrive. Something wasn't right. I had learned a long time before to recognize God's nudging me toward awareness when a situation wasn't as it should be. I trusted this sense completely. I told the girls to go to the intersection and herded them in front of me. Meanwhile, I kept a lookout behind us, which was where I believed the danger was. The nice thing about having an eccentric personality is when you ask for strange behavior, no one thinks twice about it. The group calmly went to the intersection and patiently waited for more directions.

All I could see behind us was a beautiful woman walking our way. Now let me repeat, she was stunning. She had two-inch spike heels, nice legs, draped coat, flawless makeup, and perfect hair. I would have been deeply jealous if I hadn't determined long ago that women like me make women like her even more beautiful. Her coat and dress were black, but her shoes were bright red. Nice. I couldn't see anything or anyone threatening. I began to wonder if my instincts had been skewed by the chocolate.

At the intersection we had to wait—the girls, me, and this beautiful woman. She came very close to me—too close—and I tried to keep my eyes on the girls and straight ahead, wondering what was going to happen.

"I lost a bet, and I have to wear this all day long at Halls."

I heard in my right ear a pleasant baritone voice. Almost an angelic man's voice. I turned. Yes! She had an Adam's apple. This

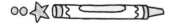 

beautiful woman was a man. He stepped through the crowd of girls and across the street with a walk that would put many women to shame. He entered Halls, and the girls stared at him and me. I just stared too, and we went to McDonald's for a debriefing.

The girls knew something was up. Although I thought the man's voice was only loud enough for my ears, the girls had heard it too. We laughed and criticized his choice of red spikes to work in all day. Then we headed home in our separate cars. During the drive I thought about what I had witnessed.

Why had my alarm bells gone off for a man in women's clothing? I turned onto the highway and listened for God's answer. I got the impression that it wasn't that the man had on women's clothing, but rather that he wasn't what he appeared to be. Then I started to see the light.

I reflected on how many times things aren't what they seem in our classrooms. Students come in completely self-assured. Parents are organized and interested. But it's all a facade. Many are really hurting, scared, and unsure. They have a bet with the world that they can carry off the charade, but often they lose. Sometimes we can see through it. That's when we need to love them and keep encouraging them.

I parked my car and went into the house. My husband wasn't going to believe this.

A Teacher's Job
Is Never Done

Jeanne Gibson

I had recently retired from teaching Sunday school, and seeing the children in church made me really miss the job. So during a recent evening service, I was trying hard to focus on the pastor's message. Too much wistfulness, I knew, would result in my making a new commitment—a commitment my health wasn't up to at the moment.

Two young boys, fifth or sixth graders I guessed, sat two seats ahead of me. Between the two of them, they probably managed to perform enough mischief in forty minutes to qualify for the *Guinness Book of World Records*.

During the song service, the boys really managed to shine, regaling everyone around and getting away with . . . well, not exactly murder, but a whole lot, considering where we were.

Jake, the younger one, began by taking a giant comb out of his pocket and using it to twist his hair into a dozen ridiculous-

looking peaks. Then he jumped up and went to the rest room, making sure everyone got a good look at his new hairdo. Not to be outdone, Matt began to blow huge bubbles with his gum; he even leaned forward to "accidentally" stick the bubbles onto the hair of the little girl ahead of him. As soon as Jake returned, Matt made his own visit to the rest room with a bubble hanging off his lip and an idiotic grin splitting his face.

If they were my kids, I thought, *I'd be marching them out to the lobby.*

(Did I mention that Jake is the pastor's youngest son?)

Together again, the two boys got to work building a stack of hymnals on Jake's outstretched palm. The stack got pretty wobbly, but luckily the books didn't crash before the boys tired of the game. I guess dropping the pile was a line even they were afraid to cross.

Jake took out two pink hairbrushes, and they settled down to brushing each other's hair, talking all the while. When their locks gleamed and looked just right, they crammed on their baseball hats and proceeded to doff them again and again to the several children who were watching them. An usher made shushing noises at them several times but finally gave up and walked away.

I began to do a slow boil.

Suddenly the two became interested in one of the songs and started singing along.

Well, I thought charitably, *they must not be all bad.*

The song had a refrain about raising your hands in the sanctuary. When we reached that line, a few people raised their hands in solemn worship.

Matt grabbed Jake's hands and jerked them into the air. Immediately Jake began shaking and waving his arms, mocking

the serious singers around him. At this point, a deacon came over and spoke to the boys.

"I wonder if they've ever heard of blasphemy," I muttered to myself.

Both boys suddenly had to go to the rest room again and came back supplied with at least a half-dozen bulletins from the table in the foyer. They lost no time in converting the stiff paper into airplanes. I had to admire their restraint; they only flew them below pew level. A few startled people looked down at their feet and bent down to pick something up.

I had to admire their restraint; they only flew them below pew level.

(If it had been up to me, the boys probably would have been tarred and feathered by this time.)

Jake then turned around to look at a clock mounted on the wall behind me. Draping both arms over the back of his pew, he let them dangle limply and stared at the clock for a while. Then he noticed me and transferred his dead-pan gaze to my face for a seemingly endless five minutes.

Jerking my head to indicate that he should turn around and behave himself accomplished nothing. The best teacher frown I could muster impressed him even less. By the time my uncomfortable ordeal ended, I knew for sure that I had lost all the angry-teacher talent I had ever possessed. I yanked a notebook out of my purse and began to jot down their misdeeds. Why I did this, I'm not really sure. Perhaps I intended to confront them or to show the evidence to their parents. Or maybe I was subconsciously planning to use the information in a magazine article.

Whatever my reason, I managed to compile quite a list before the evening ended.

Staring must have been hard work. Jake made another journey to the rest room. I say journey, because it took so long that Matt got worried and had to go and retrieve him.

Back in their seats, they found that the sermon had begun, so they listened in earnest for a minute or two before pulling out suckers and popping them quickly into their mouths. From time to time they extracted the suckers to see which of them was winning what seemed to be a race. Jake won and made a trip to the lobby to dispose of the sucker sticks. Meanwhile, Matt entertained himself and others by trying to balance his hairbrush on his forehead. An usher tapped him on the shoulder, and Matt good-naturedly surrendered the hairbrush.

Temporarily, of course.

By this time, I was so busy thinking up dire consequences for the two culprits, I had completely lost track of the sermon.

Then Matt leaned his head on the back of his pew and closed his eyes. The respite was brief. Immediately his head began to inch up over the back of the pew until, finally, it was hanging completely upside down, and his eyes popped open to stare at those behind him. Not a hint of a smile touched his mouth.

I looked into Matt's eyes and judged him harshly. The eternal destiny I envisioned for him was not good.

When the sermon ended, I stalked angrily out to my car. Playing catch in the parking lot were two familiar figures.

"Hey, guys," I called out, feeling much less civil than I sounded. "How did you like the service tonight?"

"Great," Jake replied. "I really liked that part about Peter and John praying for the lame man. I've been praying for a kid I

know at school to be healed, and he's a lot better. Isn't that neat?"

"I wonder how his folks felt," Matt said. "That guy was crippled all his life, and just all at once, he was like a different person. Pastor said he was walking and leaping and praising God. If that was me, I'd have me some fun, going around shocking people that I could walk again and jumping all over the place. God must really love when people do something like that."

My anger melted as it ran headlong into their childlike faith and acceptance of the evening's message.

"I'll bet you would, Matt; I'll bet you would. Good night, kids," I said and went on to my car, wondering just who had really heard the sermon that night.

The Word Is Moot

Patricia Anne Caliguire

Poor Mr. Steves. It's not that we didn't like him or his class. We did. But it was the last day of school before Christmas vacation, and studying English was the furthest thing from our minds. Half of us hadn't done our homework, and the other half weren't paying attention to Mr. Steves at all. We all hoped he wouldn't call on us that day.

In addition to our extensive writing projects that year, we had been given vocabulary assignments. Once a week Mr. Steves would either give us a written vocabulary quiz, or he would pop an oral quiz and call on us individually to stand up and use the designated words in sentences.

It must have been because we seemed so listless on the day before vacation that he chose an oral quiz. One by one we stood, and a few fortunate students were able to form passable sentences

 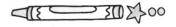

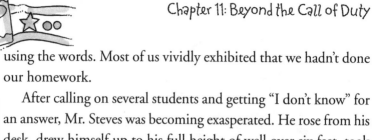

using the words. Most of us vividly exhibited that we hadn't done our homework.

After calling on several students and getting "I don't know" for an answer, Mr. Steves was becoming exasperated. He rose from his desk, drew himself up to his full height of well over six feet, took a deep breath, and began pacing back and forth in front of our desks. Finally he stopped and stared at us with a frown we knew meant trouble.

"Do you know," he thundered at last, "that all of you are in this class because you have an IQ of at least 131? It's true! But I see no evidence of any high IQs in this class today. Surely you can do better than this! Haven't any of you done your homework?"

I shrank down in my seat, praying he wouldn't call on me, since I was guilty of this offense. Usually I did well in composition and vocabulary, but lately I had been so busy with extracurricular activities and getting ready for my favorite holiday that I had begun to let my studying slide a bit. Surely Mr. Steves wouldn't notice me and would call on someone else this time.

But just as he turned to another part of the classroom to call on the next student, and I thought I could relax a bit, he suddenly looked toward the row of desks where I was sitting. Sure enough, he called on me.

I rose slowly and stood very still, hoping and praying he would ask for a word I could remember how to use in a sentence.

"Miss Martin," Mr. Steves bellowed, "please use the word *moot* in a sentence."

I groaned inwardly. I knew I should know the word and how to use it, but I drew a complete blank. However, I couldn't bear to say, "I don't know"; so I thought I'd at least try for a sentence that made sense.

"We're waiting, Miss Martin," Mr. Steves prompted.

I felt everyone's eyes on me. Cringing inside and knowing I was using the word incorrectly, I said, "The cow needed to be milked, so she moot."

The class burst into gales of laughter, and I'll never forget the look of consternation on Mr. Steves's face.

"Quiet!" he shouted, trying to regain control of the class.

Although I wanted to laugh too, I felt terrible because I knew he expected me to do better than that. Then his face melted into a grin, and he collapsed into the chair behind his desk. To our surprise he began laughing along with the rest of us!

When the commotion started to die down, Mr. Steves decided we would call it a day.

"All right," he said with a good-natured grin. "I think what we need is a vacation. It's almost time to leave, so get your things together and go ahead. However, when we return in January, Miss Martin will know how to use the word *moot* in a sentence!"

That set us off on more peals of giggling, and we gathered up our books and winter coats and hurried out the door before Mr. Steves could change his mind. Whether I would learn how to properly use that word over the course of Christmas vacation was another question. But you might say the answer was moot.

Through a
Student's Eyes

That's a Funny-Looking Pizza
EMILY MORAN

In my second-grade reading class, we were studying D words. As I held up a picture of a domino, I asked, "Does anyone know what a domino is?"

With one voice, the class answered, "Pizza."

Married to Mr. Celebrity

Jeanne Zornes

Sometimes it's hard to be married to a celebrity. I want to rip off my sunglasses and shed my bodyguards and just be me. All my married life I've been known as his wife.

The ink was still drying on our marriage license when the fans showed up on our front porch.

"Is this the house of Mr. Zornes?" How could they miss it? His name was on the mailbox.

"Is he home?" Sorry, little fan, he escaped to the hardware store. Celebrities get tired of hanging around for fans. Disappointment filled their young eyes as they slumped away and got back on their bikes.

Some fans were bolder.

"I knew him in third grade," said one middle-school student. "Could he sign this?" She held out an order blank for her soccer club's fund-raiser . . .

"Would my autograph do?" I asked. It only cost me $12.65 to substitute my signature for his, plus we'd get a tub of cookie dough in a few weeks.

Ordinary business life gets even harder. I sympathize with those stars whose shopping habits inhabit the gossip columns. Oh, the things those columnists could write about my expeditions to Goodwill and the surplus grocery outlet. Is that shopper on the other side of the frozen waffles just checking her list or jotting down notes about my clothes? I knew I shouldn't wear my yardwork jeans in public.

"Is your husband Mr. Zornes?" the clerk asks as she processes my check.

Of course. His name's on the check too.

"I adored him in fourth grade," she adds.

His fame shadows me just about everywhere. I call the clerk's office at the courthouse in another county. She has to check something and phone back. I tell her my name.

"Are you related to that Mr. Zornes?" she asks.

Yes, there's none other so famous.

Sometimes we dare to go out in public together. Wal-Mart is hazardous.

"Hi, Mr. Zornes!" children and young adults call out.

I remember a trip to the carnival at the county fair.

"Wow, Mom, Mr. Zornes is here!" I overhear one, pointing his finger at us.

It's like celebrities don't have a real life.

I'm waiting for the phone call from somebody who wants to be our agent. Or the security company that will replace our aloof gray tiger cat with a snarling doberman and electric barbed wire. We're so vulnerable, having chosen to live on an

ordinary street of tract homes. Why, our bedroom even faces the street.

I remember the afternoon he came in the house and slumped in his recliner, asking for some iced tea and the evening paper.

"Some days I feel so old," he confessed.

"I know, dear. Your washboard abs are gone. Your hairline is retreating like the March snow in our flowerbeds. Your energetic performances for all your fans take a lot out of you."

One day he was walking home from a middle school five blocks away. He'd spent the day there. An eighth grader biked past, glanced back, and stopped.

"Oh, it's you, Mr. Zornes!" he said with awe. "I thought it was just some old guy."

Yes, you're a celebrity almost forever when you've been a teacher. When my husband retired after thirty-one years of teaching elementary physical education, he had hundreds of fans. Generations of them, in fact. He substitute teaches now. Even celebrities have to pay to put their children through college. And support the spending habits of their wives.

Once I went to the grocery store and propped my sunglasses on top of my head. I was alone, since my bodyguards had left for college. The clerk was processing my wad of coupons and glanced at my check.

"By any chance are you married to Mr. Zornes, the teacher?" she asked.

"Yes, the very one."

"Tell him hi from me," she said. "I was a Hansen. He'll remember."

She's right. Celebrity teachers hardly ever forget names. Their fans depend on it.

 145

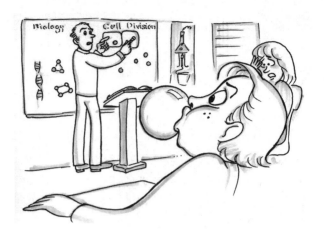

Bubblegum Woes

Patricia Anne Caliguire

It wasn't easy to fool my ninth-grade biology teacher, Mr. Pappas, but my friends had dared me to try, so I was game.

Chewing gum of any kind was verboten when I was in junior high school. Some teachers ignored it if they noticed our jaws grinding away as we slipped into class at the last minute, but some were real sticklers for the no-gum rule.

Mr. Pappas was one of the sticklers. As far as we knew, nobody had ever even tried to get away with chewing gum in his class. But at lunch one day, my friends didn't believe me when I said I could get away with it in his biology class.

Biology was my first class after lunch, so I loaded up with a good wad of Dubble Bubble and sat down calmly. This would be a piece of cake, I laughed to myself. My friends threw sharp glances at me as Mr. Pappas strode into the room.

Mr. Pappas was hard to miss. He actually stood out because he tried so hard to blend in. A slender man of medium height, Mr. Pappas wore white, short-sleeved shirts, skinny black ties, black pants, and black oxford shoes every day—that is, when he wasn't wearing brown pants with brown oxford shoes. He had a standard gold-colored watch on his left wrist and carried a large black briefcase. Every day. His dark complexion and thinning curly hair completed the look.

Mr. Pappas wasn't interested in whether his students liked him, but he did command their respect. You see, he absolutely loved biology, and he taught it with such passion that he made us want to love it too. We respected him for that. It made us want to try hard to win his respect as well.

However, as much as I respected Mr. Pappas and wanted to love biology, on this day I was going to see if I could break one of his cardinal rules and get away with it.

Mr. Pappas called the class to order and began talking about cell division. My friend Susan glanced over at me, daring me with her eyes. I kept my eyes on Mr. Pappas and started chewing as soon as he turned his back to us to write on the blackboard. As soon as he turned back to face us, I stopped chewing and kept my face blank.

This went on for some time, and I started feeling more sure of myself. He turned; I chewed. He turned back; I stopped chewing. This was too, too easy. I felt a little more daring, and this time when Mr. Pappas turned away, I blew a small bubble. As I saw him turn back, I quickly drew the bubble back into my mouth and kept my face expressionless. *He doesn't suspect a thing!* I crowed to myself.

I looked at the clock and saw that half the period was over. I was sure I could keep it up until the end of class, and I could see Susan looking at me with dismay.

I was so confident that I winked at Barbara, sitting two desks away. But it was the wink that did me in. I lost my concentration, and this time when Mr. Pappas turned around, I had blown a large bubble that just hung there as I looked at him, wide-eyed.

I expected Mr. Pappas to get mad and order me out of the room, but he said nothing. He just continued his lecture, not missing a beat. I gathered the bubble back into my mouth and chewed slowly, wondering when, or if, he'd say something.

Mr. Pappas then sat on his desk as he talked. Suddenly he stopped talking and looked straight at me. When he had said nothing for a few moments, the entire class turned around and looked at me.

"You know, I admire you," he said to me.

"You do?" I asked, wondering what was coming next.

"Yes, I really do. Do you know why?" he said, a slow smile spreading over his face.

"No," I said quietly.

He smiled broadly. "I admire you because, well, here you sit, chewing your gum, blowing bubbles. Every time you blow a bubble, all the germs that are floating around in the air of this room settle on your bubble. Then you take the bubble back into your mouth and keep on chewing, swallowing all those germs, some of which can make you ill. I admire your bravery." He shook his head, chuckling.

Feeling that he had me there, I asked, "Do you want me to get rid of my gum?"

He waved my question away. "Oh no, no, you do whatever you want with it."

He went on with his lecture as if nothing had happened, and the other students turned back to listen to him and ignored me. To save face and not let my friends think Mr. Pappas had gained the upper hand, I continued to chew my gum halfheartedly for a few minutes. Soon I became grossed out thinking about those germs I was swallowing. When no one was watching, I slipped my gum into a tissue and threw it away.

I never chewed gum in Mr. Pappas's class again. I had even more respect for him than I had before. By the way, I got an A in his class. I even learned to love biology. Imagine that!

Teaching Miss Pickle
Shae Cooke

"You can always tell Miss Pickle by her crunch!" Rebecca giggled.

"Shh, she's coming down the hall. We had better get to class," I warned.

Miss Pickle was our school principal. She also taught third grade and happened to be my teacher. She was a woman of a certain age—ninety, one hundred, one hundred and fifty? It didn't matter to me, a child of eight, going on eight-and-a-half. Old is old. Period. I'm sure when Miss Pickle was a child, there was no history class.

Her straight gray hair had a slight blue tint to it, and she wore it in a bun high atop her head. She was short—so short that she almost could have posed on top of my soccer trophy. Her onion-like skin was dry and seemed transparent, and her wrinkles were deep and furrowed. She looked a lot like Granny on *The Beverly Hillbillies*, old-fashioned and stern. She was the sort of teacher

we sat straight for, even when she just passed by in our thoughts.

"Good morning, class," she cackled.

Rebecca and I took our seats.

"Pull out your English assignments for today."

"I forgot to do it!" I whispered to my friend. A dark cloud rolled across the blank page where definitions were supposed to be. I looked up and there she stood, hands on bony hips, wearing a disappointed frown.

"I . . . I thought it was due next week, Miss Pickle."

"Miss Manuel," she replied, "you must yearn to learn. You'll stay after school to complete it."

My eyes rolled skyward. "Yes, ma'am."

After she dismissed the class, I remained at my desk and pulled out my workbook. This was going to be tough.

Miss Pickle drew up a chair beside me. "Remember what I said earlier?" she asked.

I nodded.

"What can I do to motivate you to learn and to have your assignments in on time?"

My jaw dropped. *She's asking me?* "Well, you could make learning more fun." There—I said it. I was ready to bolt. After all, Miss Pickle had been teaching for a hundred years; who was I to tell her what to do?

"I see," she said. "Tell you what, you run along home now and finish your assignment there. I'll see you in class tomorrow. And thank you for your honesty."

Whoa! I walked out of the classroom dazed. This was a close encounter of the strangest kind.

When the school bell rang the following morning, we took our seats and pulled out our spelling work sheets. Miss Pickle

hadn't arrived yet, so I recited the events of the previous day for Rebecca. Our conversation came to an abrupt end, however, as music blared over our class intercom.

"What in the—" The classroom door opened, and in came Miss Pickle dressed as a . . . well, a pickle, with an oversized encyclopedia in her hand. She belted out a rendition of "The Encyclopedia Song," as sung by Jiminy Cricket on *The Mickey Mouse Club*.

"Encyclopedia," she sang. "E-N-C-Y-C-L-O-P-E-D-I-A. You just look inside this book and you will see, every letter here from A to Z. Encyclopedia. E-N-C-Y-C-L-O-P-E-D-I-A!"

The students looked at one another in shock, but then laughter overcame us and we gave her a long round of applause.

Miss Pickle winked and smiled at me. From that day on, she had my complete devotion and attention. I admired the courage it took for her to stand in front of a class, at a hundred and fifty years old, and sing—especially in a pickle outfit. I loved the fact that she cared about us enough to go to such lengths to ensure that we enjoyed learning, and I became eager to perform well. If Miss Pickle would go that far, I certainly didn't want to let her down by not doing my very best.

Mrs. Morose and the Junglegym

Dena Dyer

As a child I was known as a teacher's pet because I got straight As, turned everything in on time, and strived to obey. In other words, I tried hard to be perfect. However, I do have several memories of teachers disciplining me. The most vivid memory involves Mrs. Morose and a curly slide.

To understand the importance of a curly slide—the kind that starts way up high and twists and turns like a roller coaster—you have to realize that I grew up in Dumas, Texas. There, the most exciting event all year was when the Lions Club members rolled up that year's sweetheart in meat-packing paper (seriously) the night before the annual barbecue.

Anyway, after a day spent inside studying—or, rather, listening to the construction crew work on our new playground—Mrs. Morose selected me, along with several other kids, to go outside and check the progress. We were instructed to glance at

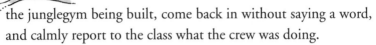
the junglegym being built, come back in without saying a word, and calmly report to the class what the crew was doing.

But when we saw the slide, we couldn't contain our joy. Along with the other students, I jumped up and down, clapping my hands and shouting, "A curly slide! A curly slide!"

Faster than the Lions Club could tenderize a beauty queen, Mrs. Morose was at my side with a ruler in hand. She grabbed my elbow and steered me toward the door, hissing, "I told you to look quietly at the playground! You'll be punished for this!"

And we were. We had to stay after school, writing something like, "I will obey my teacher and not get excited about things kids naturally get excited about" on the blackboard one hundred times.

I'm not bitter. Really, I'm not.

The redeeming part of this story is that I learned something: I wasn't a perfect student, and there are no perfect teachers. But somehow we still bumbled through, and we eventually had great fun on the junglegym.

This Is What It's All About

Students Count
BIANCA ELLIOTT

I don't teach subjects; I teach students.

Bill

David Wright

I first met William Hillary Smith in my eighth-grade class.

Teaching eighth grade is unlike teaching any other grade. It's a world of its own. A teacher who teaches eighth grade for too long can get stuck there, like a kind of purgatory. And a teacher who's stuck there for too long can begin to change. His humanity can become chipped, cracked, crushed like ground diamonds. His humor can become twisted, sarcastic, even mean. After all, eighth-grade students are not entirely human. You'll see what I mean as you read about my experiences teaching Bill.

Gum

Bill sat in the front row, his jaws working in the all-too-familiar fashion.

"Bill," I called out above the din of thirty pubescent voices. "Are you chewing gum?"

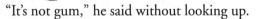

"It's not gum," he said without looking up.

"What are you chewing, Bill?"

Bill chewed twice more before answering. "Something I found."

Paper

"Do you have paper, Mr. Wright?"

"Bring your own supplies, Bill," I spoke mechanically before producing two sheets from my drawer. "Lined or unlined?"

"It doesn't matter."

I handed him the lined paper. "This is my last lined sheet, so try to be neat."

Bill put the sheet to his nose and blew. A groan of disgust erupted from the girls in the class. Bill showed his handiwork to his new audience and then to me.

"Neat enough?"

Benching Three-Fifty

"How much can you bench, Mr. Wright?"

"Oh, I don't know. About two hundred, I guess."

"That's it?" Bill shrugged his narrow shoulders. "I can bench three-fifty." There was a wild gleam in his eye.

I looked at his scrawny legs and scanned the rest of his ninety-eight-pound frame.

"I can see that."

Hunger

"Man, was I hungry yesterday!" Bill said through a mouthful of chow mein.

"Not as hungry as me," another student countered. "I went

straight home after school and ate the fridge."

Not to be bested, Bill declared, "My fridge was empty, so I cleaned out the cupboards. I mean I ate everything, even the salt."

The other boy looked at Bill and snorted through his nose. "Now that's funny."

The Schedule

"Bill, where's your schedule?"

Bill began to flip through papers in his backpack. This young man had become my personal project over the past year, and despite the apparent lack of progress in his personal development, I doggedly refused to give up.

"What are you chewing, Bill?" Bill chewed twice more before answering. "Something I found."

I watched as Bill rifled vainly through his forty-pound bag before I interrupted him.

"No, Bill. I already know you don't have one. You lost it last week. I want you to take this one."

I handed him the schedule, a coil-bound, flashy thing that cost the school $9.63 per student (including tax).

"Write down your homework assignment before you go."

"Oh, ah, OK, ah, my pen is in here somewhere." He delved back into the black hole of his school bag and did not emerge again until the end of class.

"Bill," I called out as the students began to hustle out the door. "Hold on. Show me your schedule."

"Oh, ah." He looked over his desk, in his desk, and shoved his face back in his bag.

"Bill, where is your schedule?"

"I don't know. I think someone stole it." Bill shrugged his shoulders, completely baffled.

To my credit, I did not lose my cool. I guess the years of training and experience as a schoolteacher had sufficiently prepared me for eighth-grade boys, or perhaps my subconscious common sense realized the hopelessness of the situation. Perhaps not. I grabbed the last of the extra schedules off the bookshelf, flipped to the eighth of May and wrote, "English—p. 64, questions 1–5."

Bill took the schedule, dropped it in his portable black hole, and left the room.

I flopped down behind my desk and sighed long and hard. It was Friday, 3:00 p.m., and the year was almost over. I looked at the foot-high pile of papers waiting for the attention of my nasty red pen and sighed again. Before I could begin, there was a knock at the door. A middle-aged lady appeared in the doorway with a polite, shy smile. She looked familiar, but I couldn't quite place her.

"I'm sorry to bother you," she said.

"Not at all. Come in. I was just about to start marking these papers, and I'd welcome any distraction."

She paused for a second, obviously unsure of how to take my joke. Teacher humor is not readily understood by all. I stood up and extended my hand. "I'm Mr. Wright."

She shook my hand meekly and smiled again. "I'm Mrs. Smith, Bill's mother." She stood for an awkward moment before continuing. "I was wondering if I could have a student schedule, you know, the coil-bound ones with the flashy picture on the front."

My eyebrows must have gone up because she hurried to explain. "Bill lost his on the way down to the car, and he was too afraid to ask for another one."

 160

In that moment I gained a new understanding of life and teaching. Although it was hard being Bill's teacher, or even Bill's mother, it was infinitely harder being Bill.

Nondairy Drink

When teachers stand before a class with the lesson bubbling up in their minds and out of their mouths, chalk, and fingers, they see the class as a whole. They see the boy chewing gum and sticking it under the edge of his seat. They see the glazed look of the girl in the back row. Sometimes they can even read minds. But all of this registers only in the back of their minds because more than anything else, at that moment, they want the lesson to be born, to come forth, and to be understood.

And so it is understandable that when the first student opened the brown carton and tasted its contents, I said nothing, nor did I react to the peculiar expression that came over Bill's face. I kept right on teaching.

"The past participle of *swim* is *swum*."

The words rolled off my tongue as my hands performed the completely independent action of writing the word on the board. It's hard to believe, really, that the mind is able to perform both functions at the same time.

When I turned back to face the class, I saw that the carton was in the hands of another student who was now drinking and shaking her head and making the same peculiar expression Bill had just made. By the time I finished the list of ten past participles, the carton had passed to that many students, all of whom made the same rather bewildering face, and back to Bill.

"Enough!" I exclaimed.

It's important to explain, at this point, that when a teacher's ire has been aroused, it is not generally because of a broken rule, a careless mistake, or even a student's open disregard for the fine institution of education. On the contrary, it's usually because of the limp and lifeless body of a stillborn lesson that lies at his feet, a lesson that only moments before had appeared so alive and vital in his mind. And so, with righteous indignation, like Christ in the temple, I vented my wrath.

"Bill!"

Bill's face reddened with fear.

"What is that drink doing in this class? You know full well that there is no drinking allowed in class, except for water." I took two giant strides across the room and wrested the carton from Bill's trembling fingers. All eyes were on him as I raised the mysterious brown carton and read the label.

I took two giant strides across the room and wrested the carton from Bill's trembling fingers.

It was an epiphany—the brown carton, the sour faces, and the inquisitive attention from the other students in the class. In my mind's eye, I saw Bill at the local convenience store buying what he thought to be a carton of chocolate milk, not bothering to read the label.

"Nondairy Mocha Whitener," I said by way of explanation. "You put this in your coffee like cream and sugar." I smiled down at Bill. "Would you like me to get you a cup of coffee to go with your Nondairy Mocha Whitener?" My voice dripped with condescension.

Bill looked up and smiled back.

"Why, yes. That would be wonderful."

Love at First Sight

Bill was now in high school, and so was I. We were studying *Romeo and Juliet*, that fateful tale of prejudice, hatred, and young, unbridled love. Could this medieval tale from the pages of history and the pen of Shakespeare possibly have lessons for the modern teenager? At one time in the distant past, as a confident, young, idealistic teacher, I had believed it could.

"Do you believe in love at first sight?" I asked the class tentatively. I received the worst of all answers—silence. Teaching can be a miserable, unrewarding job. But every once in a while, a student like Bill comes along who makes it all worthwhile. It's almost as if you can see the light bulb go on, and instead of folly, wisdom pours from his mouth like a cool, clear spring.

"I think . . . ," Bill began, and my eyes widened involuntarily.

Bill had said many things over the past six months. He'd told the class his bunny's name was Putrid, that his house was made of Jell-O, and that he ate spiders for dinner. But as far as I could remember, Bill had never attempted to talk about literature. For the first time in a long time, I saw a glimmer of light in a cold, dark universe.

"I think," Bill continued, "love at first sight is not a good idea. Romeo may be a maniac killer. He could have a big knife and could come after Juliet in the middle of the night while she's sleeping." He paused meditatively with his finger on his chin. "The end result of this could be divorce."

I made a mental note not to call on Bill for any more thought-provoking responses in the future.

Rainy-Day Field Trip

Four out of thirty-one students showed up for the annual twelfth-grade nature walk on a rainy day in June. Bill was one of the four. It had been years since I first taught Bill, and many things had changed.

Bill was never a problem in class anymore. In fact, he rarely spoke at all. His assignments were always done on time, and he never missed a class, which was quite an achievement in this part of town. It was hard even to associate the scrawny, scatter-brained eighth grader with this tall young man who walked patiently through the puddles before him. But there they were, grade-eight Bill and grade-twelve Bill, one and the same. Although I had seen this transformation many times in my twenty years of teaching, Bill was a special case that had particularly tested my faith. Yet somehow, magically, the impossible had happened. Bill had grown up.

The students walked through the rain for three hours. There was no place to go until the bus picked them up, so on we trod with nothing but sparse cedars for cover and the poetic ramblings of long-dead Romantics for entertainment. By the end of the trip, the students were four cold, soaked bundles of silence.

I had never expected much from the field trip. It always looked good on paper, to read the nature poets—Keats, Shelley, and Wordsworth—while surrounded by nature; but it was rarely well attended, and most students who had made it all the way to twelfth-grade honors English cared about little but marks. I certainly didn't expect what I read in Bill's writing journal the next day.

Ode to a Rained-Out Field Trip
William Hillary Smith

The rain is like a friend, you know, a friend that is like me.
The sun could never be my friend that way, not now.
It rained the day I lost myself, the day I started school.
It rained the day I lost my soul, the day my mother died.
Now it rains every day and that is cool 'cause,
well, rain's what I have left.
It's all that I have left.

Teachers spend their careers—have nervous breakdowns, drink gallons of coffee—all trying to make an impossible kid learn and grow up. Then one day, before you know it, he does. But as I sat there that afternoon, I would have given up my teacher's pension just to hear one more story about Bill.

The Good Old Days?

Martha Bolton

"Children today are tyrants. They contradict their parents, gobble their food and tyrannize their teachers."

The above quote wasn't said by William Bennett, President George W. Bush, Laura Bush, or any other leader of our time. It was spoken by Socrates, a philosopher who doesn't get around much on the speaking circuit these days. (I think his speaking fees are a little on the pricey side.)

Considering what he said, though, it would seem that things haven't changed a whole lot since his day. Apparently, kids were trying to push the limits even back then.

"Son, we need to talk. Your teacher said you were popping wheelies with the chariot again."

"I don't care if your schoolbooks do feel like stone tablets, Cornelius. If you've got homework to do, it's your responsibility to bring 'em home!"

"I can't wear these sandals, Mom. They're so 500 BC."

"Get a job? No one's hiring, and there's no way I'm gonna shepherd for minimum wage!"

"Don't use that tone of voice with me, young lady! Now, I'm telling you for the last time, if that toga doesn't come to your knees, you're not wearing it!"

Sound familiar? Every generation thinks its trends, fashion sense, and attitudes are original. But if they'd do a little research, they'd discover there isn't anything new about them. That cutting-edge look they're so proud of has simply come full circle. Fashion loves to repeat itself. This year long hair is in. Next year long hair is out. The next year it's back in again. Short skirts are in this season, out next season, and back in the following season. And bad attitudes aren't anything new either.

When we start thinking today's youth are hopeless, it might help us to remember Socrates. Maybe he didn't have to put up with a rock band practicing in the garage next door, but there had to have been a teenager or two on his block really getting on his nerves. Why else would he say what he said? He doesn't provide a lot of explanation along with it, but we can certainly speculate that the philosopher had his share of teenagers around who were bucking authority.

So maybe returning to the good old days isn't our answer after all. Maybe what we need is for each generation to teach its young people the importance of believing in and bringing out the best in themselves and others and instill in them an unshakable faith that they will survive no matter what life brings their way. And to keep a good sense of humor about it all.

Source Notes

Chapter 1: Starting Out

"S-E-X" taken from *Christian Reader* (January/February 1996). Copyright © 1996 by Linda Strater. Used by permission.

"Confessions of a Student Teacher" by Jeanne Zornes. Copyright © 2004. Used by permission.

"First Day of School" by Teresa Bell Kindred. Copyright © 2004. Used by permission.

"Meet the Teacher" by Joni Woodward. Copyright © 2004. Used by permission.

Chapter 2: Out of the Mouths of Babes

"Mrs. Teacher" by Mary Ann Bertram. Copyright © 2004. Used by permission.

"Jesus, Kids, and Me" by Dena Dyer. Copyright © 2004. Used by permission.

"Grandma's Creation" taken from *Christian Reader* (May/June 2002). Copyright © 2002 by Gary Crandall. Used by permission.

"Look Who's Watching" by Linda Gilden. Copyright © 2004. Used by permission.

"Hark! The Herald Preschoolers Sing" taken from the *Church Advocate* (December 1989). Copyright © 1989 by Bob Welch. Used by permission.

"Preschool Germs" by Cindy Thomson. Copyright © 2004. Used by permission.

Chapter 3: Kindergarten Capers

"No Cheating!" taken from *Christian Reader* (May/June 2002). Copyright © 2002 by Margo Taylor. Used by permission.

"Give Your Best" by Linda Gilden. Copyright © 2004. Used by permission.

"Undies" taken from *Christian Reader* (September/October 2000). Copyright © 2000 by Amy Jenkins. Used by permission.

"The Calm before the Storm" by Mary Horner Collins. Copyright © 2004. Used by permission.

"What Do You Want to Be?" by James McCullen. Copyright © 2004. Used by permission.

"Holy Moses" by Sharon Hinck. Copyright © 2004. Used by permission.

Chapter 4: It's Elementary, My Dear

"Sad Face" taken from *Christian Reader* (March/April 2003). Copyright © 2003 by Jo Ann Cook. Used by permission.

"Do You Live Here?" by Kari Ziman. Copyright © 2004. Used by permission.

"How to Destroy Graven Images" by Silvana Clark.

Copyright © 2004. Used by permission.

"The Skinny on Ants" taken from *Christian Reader* (November/December 1999). Copyright © 1999 by Amy Jenkins. Used by permission.

"Spare Sodom?" taken from *Christian Reader* (May/June 2003). Copyright © 2003 by Lois Bergy. Used by permission.

"Liar, Liar" by Len Woods. Copyright © 2004. Used by permission.

Chapter 5: Middle-School Madness

"A Gaseous State" taken from *Christian Reader* (May/June 1995). Copyright © 1995 by Jack Eppolito. Used by permission.

"That Old Sew-and-Sew," originally titled "We Aren't Valued," taken from *Choosing the Amusing* by Marilyn Meberg. Copyright © 1999. Reprinted by permission, Word Publishing, Nashville, Tennessee. All rights reserved.

"Redhead Prejudice" by Bianca Elliott. Copyright © 2004. Used by permission.

"The Whichit" by Deedee Muehlbauer. Copyright © 2004. Used by permission.

"Opera" by Jennifer Blaske. Copyright © 2004. Used by permission.

Chapter 6: High-School Happenings

"Too Old for This Job" by Teresa Bell Kindred. Copyright © 2004. Used by permission.

"If the Shoe Fits" by Amy Davidson Grubb. Copyright © 2004. Used by permission.

"The Hormone Challenge" by Teresa Bell Kindred. Copyright © 2004. Used by permission.

"Homework Hassles" taken from *The Dog Ate It* by Elaine K.

McEwan. Copyright © 1996 by Elaine K. McEwan-Adkins. Published by Harold Shaw Publishers. Used by permission.

Chapter 7: Stick to the Subject

"Hands Off" taken from *Christian Reader* (January/February 2001). Copyright © 2001 by Jim Voller. Used by permission.

"Embellied" by Dalene Vickery Parker. Copyright © 2004. Used by permission.

"You Call That History?" by Teresa Bell Kindred. Copyright © 2004. Used by permission.

"Discerning Minds Want to Know" by Elizabeth Delayne. Copyright © 2004. Used by permission.

"Spelling Lesson" by Kathryn Lay. Copyright © 2004. Used by permission.

Chapter 8: Those Amazing Subs

"Any Volunteers?" taken from *Christian Reader* (March/April 1995). Copyright © 1995 by Margaret N. Windley. Used by permission.

"How Hard Can This Be?" by Margolyn Woods. Copyright © 2004. Used by permission.

"Classroom Riot" by Amber Ferguson. Copyright © 2004. Used by permission.

"Which Witch?" by Marti Kramer Suddarth. Copyright © 2004. Used by permission.

"Second-Grade Theology" by Elaine Mitchell. Copyright © 2004. Used by permission.

Chapter 9: Of Parents and Principals

"Be Nice" taken from *Christian Reader* (January/February 2000). Copyright © 2000 by Doris Johnson. Used by permission.

"The Apple Doesn't Fall Far" by Brenda Nixon. Copyright © 2004. Used by permission.

"Tuna Yule" taken from *Christian Reader* (November/December 2000). Copyright © 2000 by Karen Cogan. Used by permission.

"In the Office with Jason" taken from *Nobody Likes Me* by Elaine K. McEwan. Copyright © 1996 by Elaine K. McEwan-Adkins. Published by Harold Shaw Publishers. Used by permission.

"Smoking in the Boys' Room" by Laurie Copeland. Copyright © 2004. Used by permission.

Chapter 10: There Are Bad Days... and Then There's Teaching

"Pet Peeves" taken from *Christian Reader* (September/October 1992). Copyright © 1992 by Anita Donihue. Used by permission.

"The Bug in the Basement" by Carol Chaffee Fielding. Copyright © 2004. Used by permission.

"Trailer Living" by Teresa Bell Kindred. Copyright © 2004. Used by permission.

"Standing Ovation" by Bianca Elliott. Copyright © 2004. Used by permission.

"The Sharpening Demon" by Brandy S. Brow. Copyright © 2004. Used by permission.

"The Bomb Exercise" by Len Woods. Copyright © 2004. Used by permission.

Chapter 11: Beyond the Call of Duty

"The Mark of a Teacher" taken from *Christian Reader* (November/December 1995). Copyright © 1995 by David L. Roper. Used by permission.

"Frosty Chaperone" by Teresa Bell Kindred. Copyright © 2004. Used by permission.

"Things Aren't What They Seem" by Bianca Elliott. Copyright © 2004. Used by permission.

"A Teacher's Job Is Never Done" by Jeanne Gibson. Copyright © 2004. Used by permission.

"The Word Is Moot" by Patricia Anne Caliguire. Copyright © 2004. Used by permission.

Chapter 12: Through a Student's Eyes

"That's a Funny Looking Pizza" taken from *Christian Reader* (May/June 1991). Copyright © 1991 by Emily Moran. Used by permission.

"Married to Mr. Celebrity" by Jeanne Zornes. Copyright © 2004. Used by permission.

"Bubblegum Woes" by Patricia Anne Caliguire. Copyright © 2004. Used by permission.

"Teaching Miss Pickle" by Shae Cooke. Copyright © 2004. Used by permission.

"Mrs. Morose and the Junglegym" by Dena Dyer. Copyright © 2004. Used by permission.

Chapter 13: This Is What It's All About

"Students Count" by Bianca Elliott. Copyright © 2004. Used by permission.

"Bill" by David Wright. Copyright © 2004. Used by permission.

"The Good Old Days?" taken from *I Think, Therefore I Have a Headache* by Martha Bolton. Copyright © 2003 by Martha Bolton. Published by Bethany House Publishers, a division of Baker Book House Company. Used by permission.

Contributors

Lois Bergy has been teaching junior church for forty-three years. Her story, "Sparing Sodom," is just one of a myriad of memories.

Mary Ann Bertram has been a Spanish teacher for more than thirty years. She is a mother of three and is involved in the Orthodox Church.

Jennifer Blaske is a music teacher and freelance writer who admits listening to Fleetwood Mac and the Monkees much more than to opera. Although she loved her experience working in the public schools, today she gives private music lessons in her home so she can spend more time with her two daughters, Rachael and Rebecca, and her husband, Robert. She lives in metro Atlanta.

Martha Bolton is a full-time comedy writer and the author of more than fifty books. She was a staff writer for Bob Hope for fifteen years and has written for Phyllis Diller, Ann Jillian, and many others.

She has received four Angel Awards, an Emmy nomination, and a Dove Award nomination.

Brandy S. Brow is a homeschooling mother of five and the *Busy Homeschool* editor for Busy Parents Online. She is also the founder and director of Pioneer Academy, a Vermont private school for homeschooling families. In her spare time, she writes articles and stories along with her homeschool column, "Homeschool Daze: Medicine for Home Educators."

Patricia Anne Caliguire is a freelance Christian writer and speaker who enjoys writing articles, stories, and essays that uplift and inspire. Patricia and her family live in Valrico, Florida.

Silvana Clark turned her expertise in creating graven images into material for two craft books. As a professional business speaker, she incorporates humor, games, and, yes, even crafts into her presentations. Happily married for twenty-seven years, Silvana writes about her husband's creative parenting ideas. She gets the credit for being the author of five parenting books while he does the work.

Karen Cogan enjoys writing inspirational stories and articles as well as romantic fiction. She is the author of a recently released novel, *The Secret of Castlegate Manor*, published by Avalon Books.

Mary Horner Collins has taught music, served on staff with InterVarsity Christian Fellowship for five years, and worked in Christian publishing for more than twelve years. She is currently an editor for The Livingstone Corporation in Carol Stream, Illinois. She lives in New Hampshire and is grateful for her loving husband, gifted stepdaughter, and adorable cat.

Jo Ann Cook is a freelance writer and former schoolteacher. She resides in Dublin, Georgia, with her husband, Harry.

Shae Cooke is a native of Montreal who currently resides in British Columbia. An inspirational writer, she is also a mother and former foster child who shares her heart and God's message of hope in publications worldwide. At the moment, she is busy working on two nonfiction books, *Prime Time with the Lord* and *Devotions by the Jarful.*

Laurie Copeland comes from a long line of teachers. As a matter of fact, the Bill Barker she speaks of in her story is her father. Laurie is a teacher of another sort: she is a speaker, writer, and actress. Laurie and her husband, John, have one child, Kailey, and live in Longwood, Florida.

Gary Crandall has been a pastor for twenty-five years and is the author of *Gold Under Fire: The Christian and Adversity.*

Elizabeth Delayne teaches social studies in the middle-Georgia area. She graduated from Hardin-Simmons University in Abilene, Texas, with a degree in history and speech communication. Her Web site, www.edelayne.com, provides free-to-read online inspirational romances. Outside of teaching and writing, she can be found photographing historical sites.

Anita Corrine Donihue is a pastor's wife, mother, and grandmother, and teaches elementary-age children with special needs. Anita is author of *When I'm on My Knees* and a book series on prayer.

Dena Dyer started writing for publication as a preteen and received a bachelor's degree in vocal music and professional writing from Baylor University in 1993. She is a professional writer, actress, and singer with credits in more than 140 magazines. She has also contributed to several books, including *Rest Stops for Busy Moms, The Heart of a Mother, The Art of Helping, Simple*

Pleasures of Friendship, and *Divine Stories of the Yahweh Sisterhood*.

Bianca Elliott recently celebrated her tenth year of service in the same public school district. She taught middle school for five years and currently teaches in the high school.

Amber Ferguson homeschools her children while managing a small construction office. Winner of three contests for humorous writing, she freelances as both a writer and a graphic artist—defiantly snickering whenever her doctor advises eight hours of sleep. From her desk chair, Amber enjoys an inspiring view of Lake Livingston, Texas, where she lives a blessed life with her husband and two children.

Carol Chaffee Fielding and her husband, Bruce, spent ten years teaching at a boarding school. Carol is currently a stay-at-home mother, homeschooling her three daughters Caitlin, Amanda, and Ailee.

Jeanne Gibson, a former junior high school English and math teacher, lives in Springfield, Oregon, with her husband, Malcolm, and their frisky cat, Snoopy. Her writing has appeared in *Mature Years*, *Jack and Jill*, *Leadership*, *Junior High School Teacher*, and *Sunday Digest*.

Linda Gilden is the author of numerous articles appearing in publications such as *Focus on the Family*, *HomeLife*, *Family Fun*, *The Lookout*, and *Discipleship Journal*. She has also contributed to nine books, including *Every Child Is a Winner*, and serves as managing editor of *The Encourager*. Linda and her husband enjoy family time, where she finds lots of inspiration for her writing!

Amy Davidson Grubb taught high-school Latin for five years and now teaches English at Germanna Community College in

Fredericksburg, Virginia. She is also writing a young-adult novel, *Even the Sparrow*, a work of historical fiction set in the Depression-era South. She lives in Fredericksburg with her husband, Robert, and their two children, Adam and Mary Kate.

Sharon Hinck is a wife and mother of four. She has a master's degree in communications and is currently writing a series of fantasy novels about a soccer mom following God's call during adventures in an alternate world.

Amy Jenkins writes articles, humor, and narrative nonfiction. A lover of anthologies, she manages the Web site www.anthologiesonline.com and has been published in multiple compilations.

Teresa Bell Kindred is a wife and mother of five children. A former high-school history teacher with a master's degree in secondary education, she now writes magazine columns for *Kentucky Living* and *Rhyme and Reason*. She has authored four Precious Moments gift books, a self-help book on dealing with stress, and *Mozart for a Mother's Soul*. She is also a conference and retreat speaker.

Kathryn Lay is a freelance writer and homeschool mom living in Texas with her daughter and husband, a public school teacher. Her writing has appeared in hundreds of books and magazines, including *Woman's Day*, *Guideposts*, *Kiwanis*, *Chicken Soup for the Mother's Soul*, and *Chocolate for a Woman's Courage*. One of Kathryn's greatest joys is seeing children get excited about reading.

James McCullen retired in 2001 after forty years of full-time pastoral work. The following Sunday he began a part-time pastorate in Belgrade, Missouri, and commenced a writing career. He now writes a weekly commentary for the *Pathway News*

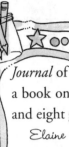

Journal of the Missouri Baptist Convention and has also written a book on prayer. He and his wife, Christa, have two daughters and eight grandchildren.

Elaine K. McEwan, EdD, is a former teacher and administrator who has written more than twenty-five books in the fields of child rearing and education. Some of her volumes include: *Teach Them All to Read*, *The Principal's Guide to Raising Math Achievement*, and *Seven Steps to Effective Instructional Leadership*. She travels nationwide, offering training on how teachers and administrators can raise reading achievement.

Marilyn Meberg loves life, people, and God's Word. A popular speaker and author of many titles, including *The Zippered Heart*, *Choosing the Amusing*, and *I'd Rather be Laughing*, Marilyn has a master's degree in English and taught at Biola University for ten years. With a second master's in counseling psychology, Marilyn decided to start another career helping people. In addition, she is a vibrant member of the speaking team for the Women of Faith conferences.

Elaine Mitchell resides in Dresden, Ohio, and is a spiritual-retreat director and a member of Christian Writers Fellowship International.

Deedee Muehlbauer is a former middle-school language arts teacher with a master's degree in education. When not acting as a nurse, short-order cook, referee, and keeper of all knowledge for her two children, she works as a consultant to computer companies and has written technical manuals, drama scripts, and a weekly column for a local newspaper.

Brenda Nixon's desire as a speaker, author, and educator is to build healthier families through parent empowerment. She is the author of a book on raising young children, *Parenting Power in*

the Early Years. Brenda lives in Ohio with her husband, two daughters, a miniature dachshund, and a brat cat that is beyond discipline.

Dalene Vickery Parker is a freelance writer, editor, and speaker who lives in Spartanburg, South Carolina, with her husband and two children. She enjoys teaching high-school English, particularly to students who get excited about new words!

David L. Roper is a preacher, teacher, and writer. He currently writes full time for Truth for Today World Mission Council.

Linda Strater, married and mother of three sons, lives in beautiful Minnesota. She writes for the simple joy it brings to her and others.

Marti Kramer Suddarth is a writer and composer whose work includes *Mini-Musicals for Special Days*, *Greeblemeisers*, and *The Adventures of Quinn Quarternote and the Wooden Spoon Orchestra*. She and her husband live in southeastern Indiana with their three children, five gerbils, an anole lizard, a newt, two fire-bellied toads, and a beagle named Splash. Marti is proud of her long nose!

Margo Taylor is a retired elementary teacher, mother of two (a son and a daughter), and grandmother of six. She loves to write—especially stories, poems, and plays for children.

Cindy Thomson, a preschool and kindergarten teacher for nearly twenty years, is now an aspiring novelist. She has written pieces for *Family History* and the Society of American Baseball Research. Her opportunity to minister to nearly three hundred children over the years has provided plenty of inspiration. Mrs. Thomson lives in central Ohio with her husband and three teenage sons.

Jim Voller is a retired high-school headmaster and a writer of

short stories. His teaching career extended over thirty-eight years, during which time he was also a lay preacher.

Bob Welch is a columnist at the *Register-Guard* newspaper in Eugene, Oregon, and author of *American Nightingale* (Atria Books, 2004), about the first WWII nurse to die after the landings at Normandy. He also serves as an adjunct professor of journalism at the University of Oregon (www.bobwelch.net).

Len Woods is a husband, father, small-group leader, author, and mechanically impaired homeowner in Ruston, Louisiana. He hopes to fix his storm door sometime before the Second Coming.`

Margolyn Woods, a former Rose Bowl Queen and actress, is now a widely acclaimed speaker for women's retreats and conferences. She has written eight books, most recently *Comfort for the Grieving Heart,* published by SunCreek Books. She lives in Edmond, Oklahoma, with her husband and their three children.

Joni Woodward lives in southeast Texas. She is married to her junior-high and high-school sweetheart, and they have two wonderful sons. She taught elementary school for twelve years, where she learned that adult recognition pales when compared to a crayon drawing with the words "I love you, Mrs. Woodward" or an unexpected but heartfelt hug.

David Wright is a high-school teacher at British Columbia Christian Academy in Port Coquitlam, Canada. He has been teaching for nine years in the liberal-arts field. He is also active in his church, teaching Sunday school, leading singing, and being a general, all-purpose hamburger helper when the need arises. David is married with two daughters.

Kari Ziman and her husband, Jonathan, live in San Jose, California. Kari has taught high-school science in Tokyo and ele-

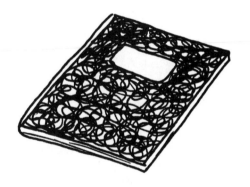

mentary school in California. She is now a stay-at-home mom, working full-time to raise her daughter, Eliana, and tutoring four days a week.

Jeanne Zornes is an educator, conference speaker, and prize-winning author of hundreds of articles and seven books, including *Spiritual Spandex for the Outstretched Soul*. She has a bachelor's degree in education from Western Washington University and a master's in communications from Wheaton College.